MW00474346

21 DAY

Daniel Fast

WORKBOOK
WITH STUDY GUIDE
MEAL PLANNERS
DEVOTIONAL
PRAYERS & MORE.

MARIA TARNEV-WYDRO, HD

"And God is able to bless you abundantly, so that in all things at all times, having all that you need, you will abound in every good work."
-2 Corinthians 9:8...Expect a miracle!

More books and info at **www.HealthyLivingMinistry.org**

www.Danielfast.org

Healthy Living
Ministry

WELCOME TO THE 21 DAY DANIEL FAST

Join us for a 21 day journey of transformation and amazing spiritual breakthroughs. We believe something powerful can happen in our lives when we set aside certain things to focus on our relationship with God. The Bible is filled with examples of God's power when his people decided to fast and concentrate on his love, grace and mercy.

Most people politely leave the room when we talk about fasting. Let's face it ... we all love to eat! The good news about the 21 Day Daniel Fast is that you can still eat all you want! During this 21-day period we're encouraging you to adopt the same diet that the prophet Daniel used in the Bible.

Why are we doing this? It is not primarily to lose weight. Of course, you will likely lose weight and feel great, but we are doing it to honor God. When we are all united in prayer and fasting, the power of God is unleashed.

The aim of this book is to guide you in planning your spiritual fasting and to give you the tools and insights to allow you to experience your own spiritual breakthroughs.

Expect a miracle!

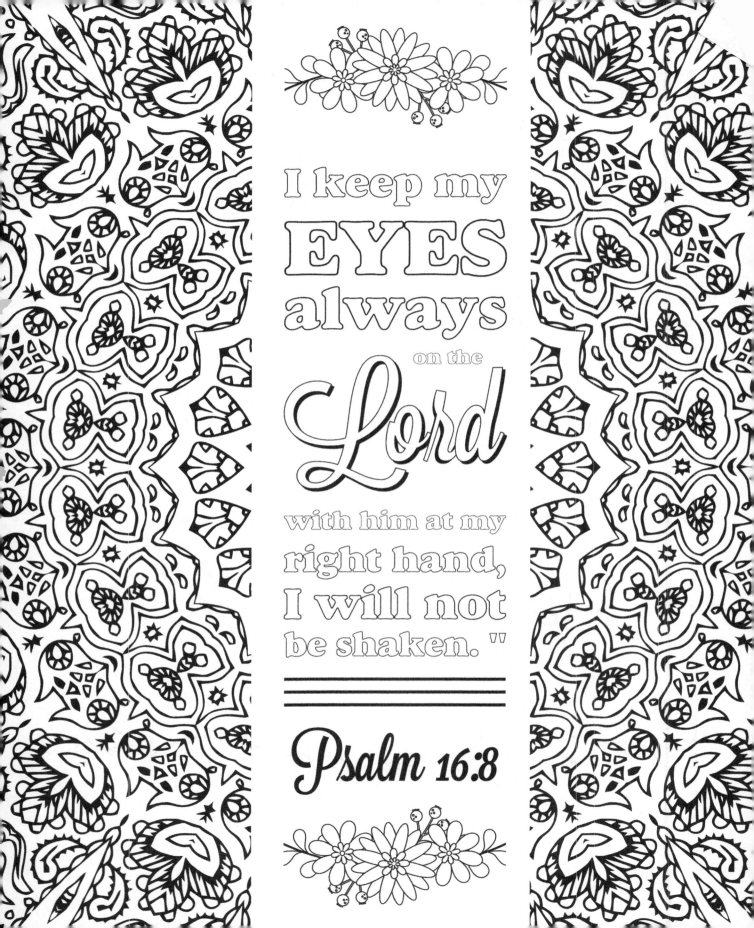

I keep my
EYES
always
on the
Lord
with him at my
right hand,
I will not
be shaken. "

Psalm 16:8

HOW TO USE THIS GUIDE

The 21 Day Daniel Fast Guide is designed to take you by the hand and lead you through this exciting time from those who have already done it. It contains daily prayers, verses, praises, Bible study chapters and even meal suggestions to make it easy for you to complete the fast. Over the course of the next 21 days you will be spending a portion of your day praying and studying God's Word. In knowing His Word you will know Him better. And in knowing Him better you can't help but want to be more like Him.

The 21 Day Daniel Fast Journal Workbook consists of 3 parts. They are:

Guiding Section – This section will teach you how to fast like Daniel by preparing yourself spiritually and physically. Please read this section with your prayer partner or group before you start fasting.

Fasting Section – This section guides you through the 21 day fast and also includes a 21 Day Devotional, Bible Study Notes, Prayer Requests, Weekly Meal Planning and Log with Shopping List, Conversation with My Lord Journaling Pages in order to record your journey in an organized fashion. It also allows you to be in sync with your fasting partners and to learn together from your experiences.

Prayer Tool Box – These are some extra tools to help you along the way. There is a Prayer Calendar, Meal Ideas, Daniel Fast Food List, FAQ, Suggested Prayers and Notes. Not only will you be able to record your thoughts, prayers and wurk with God, but also express your faith creatively through coloring each page. This is a personalized keepsake journal that you will cherish always and can refer to in time of need.

LET'S GET STARTED!

TABLE OF CONTENTS

TABLE OF CONTENTS

"SHOW ME YOUR WAYS, *Lord,* TEACH ME YOUR PATHS. GUIDE ME IN YOUR TRUTH AND TEACH ME, FOR YOU ARE GOD MY SAVIOR, AND MY HOPE IS IN *You* ALL DAY LONG."

PSALM 25:4-5

21 DAY DANIEL FAST GUIDE

"I will instruct thee and teach thee in the way which thou shalt go: I will guide thee with mine eye."

Psalms 32:8

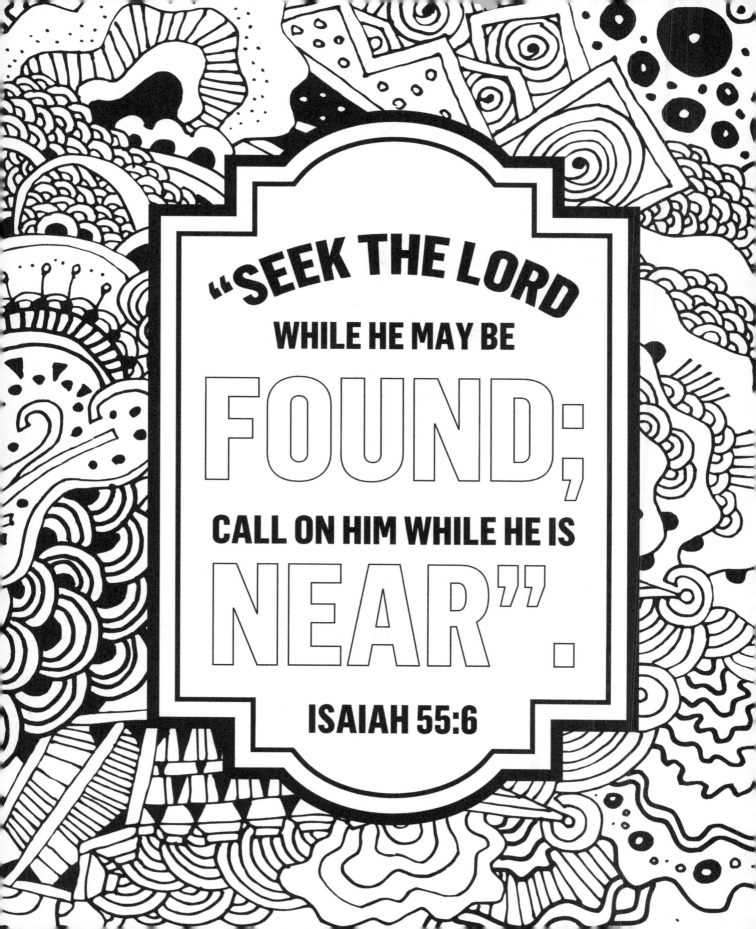

WHAT IS PRAYER?

Prayer is simply a conversation between us and God. It is our opportunity to tell God our deepest secrets and desires, to confess our sins, ask His forgiveness, thank him and to pray on behalf of others. Prayer is a time to give God praise for who He is and all He does. Prayer is also God's opportunity to speak to us. Those feelings of calm and comfort are God's telling us He is present. And when we stop talking for a while after telling God what is on our heart and mind, He will answer by placing Godly thoughts in our minds, or by answering us through other people, circumstances, or by giving us the decisions and choices we need to make.

Again...prayer is conversation and just like there are several different 'types' of conversation, there are different types of prayer. Sometimes our prayers are short, sweet, and to the point. Sometimes they are general in nature; something for everyone to hear. And then there are those prayers that are personal and private—reserved for only you and God.

"I pray because I can't help myself. I pray because I am helpless. I pray because the need flows out of me all the time – waking and sleeping. It does not change God- it changes me." - C.S. Lewis

THE PURPOSE OF PRAYER

The purpose of prayer is to establish and maintain your relationship with God—to get to know Him, to learn to trust Him, to grow your faith, to listen to God's direction and will for your life, to worship and praise Him, to lay your heart, soul, and mind completely bare before Him so that you can experience God's full measure of love, comfort, strength, wisdom, and blessing.

Prayer should be a constant in your life—not something reserved only for those times the family is gathered around the dinner table, when you are at church, or if you can stay awake long enough at night when you go to bed. And prayer certainly shouldn't be used only when you can't think of anything else to do. No, prayer should be...prayer must be a part of who you are.

You wouldn't or couldn't maintain a solid relationship with anyone else without solid and consistent communication, so why would you think it would be any different with God? Prayer should also be an 'automatic'. By automatic I don't mean recited word for word without even thinking about it. I mean it should be something you consider a must for getting through the day—even more than coffee or checking email.

THE PURPOSE OF FASTING

There are actually several different purposes or reasons for fasting. The reasons we see in the Bible for fasting include grief, focusing on God's will, worship, and as an expression or way of requesting something from God. David fasted in his grief over his infant son's illness. King Darius fasted to express his grief for having to comply with the law that required him to throw Daniel into a den of lions. The Israelites fasted as a show of grief over their sinful ways. It is a way to draw our attention or focus on God.

Moses fasted for forty days prior to receiving the Ten Commandments. Jesus fasted in the wilderness for forty days following his baptism by John the Baptist and just prior to being tempted by Satan. Anna fasted as an act of worship and praise for the baby Jesus. Saul (later, Paul) fasted for three days following his conversion for the purpose of showing his dependence and submission to Christ. Esther also fasted as an expression of humility to allow God to work through her to save the entire Jewish race. Fasting should serve the same purposes for us as it did for the people we read about in the Bible. And yes, we should fast. While there is no commandment saying, "Thou shall fast", there isn't one that says "Thou shall pray", either. But Jesus lets us know we are expected to do both when he says (in the Sermon on the Mount) when you pray and when you fast—not if.

PRAY: Father, I come to you now in preparation for this period of fasting, prayer, and Bible study. I come asking for your blessing, your strength, and your wisdom. I ask that you open my heart, soul, and mind to what you want me to learn from this time. I ask that you will make me moldable and that I will grow in faith and in my commitment to being yours. I am thankful for the amazing creation that is my body and for the testimony of Daniel that teaches me how to care for my body in a way that is more pleasing to you. In the name of Jesus I pray, Amen.

WHAT'S THE HOLY SPIRIT'S HOTLINE?
Call 1-800-P-R-A-Y-A-N-D-F-A-S-T.

Once you decide to call this hotline, you are in for a great adventure. Be ready to travel in the realm of the Spirit and experience great things like you have never experienced before. Bring a backpack because you'll surely return with plenty of favor and breakthroughs.

Some people don't pray much because they find it boring. But I guess they haven't explored the immense possibilities of prayer just yet. Prayer is a way of communicating with God through His Spirit that is alive within us. But it's more than just that. Prayer allows us to go places we have never been before. If prayer is exciting, then fasting takes the adventure to an even greater level. When we fast, we totally renounce our dependence on the flesh, allowing our Spirit to operate in full gear. Through fasting, we receive a kind of wisdom that is out of this world. We experience breakthroughs after breakthroughs and we are taken from glory to glory.

A plane during takeoff needs to run to its full power before it can break through the pull of gravity and fly. Based on reports, the plane consumes the most fuel during takeoff and climb. Likewise, when the Spirit wants to take flight in our lives, we need a lot of prayers that serve as fuel that allow us to reach a point of breakthrough.

WHAT IS FASTING?

According to the dictionary, fasting is voluntarily abstaining from food or drink for a period of time. The Hebrew word in the Bible used for fasting means to 'cover the mouth'. The Greek word used in the Bible (for fasting) means 'to abstain from food'.

Fasting is a spiritual discipline; meaning it is something we do for our spiritual lives (well-being). We fast so that we can be still before God and hear what He has to say to us. We are taking charge of our bodies rather than letting our body take charge of us.

Fasting is a sacrifice in such a way that we deny the desires of the flesh to make our Spirit stronger. Imagine turning on the volume of your speakers. The sound is distributed equally in both left and right speakers. When we are fasting, we turn down the volume of the world a few notches so that we can turn up the volume of the Spirit. The length of the fast and the intensity of our prayer will determine the Spirit's volume in our minds. The more we fast and pray, the greater the clarity of the voice of the Spirit.

Man is composed of body, soul, and spirit. As human beings living in a tangible world, we are programmed to operate in the physical realm because this is what is tangible and visible. However, the success that we can achieve in the physical realm is only limited to the things that we have control of. This is where the work of the Holy Spirit comes in.

Before Jesus' death, He promised the disciples that the Father will send the Holy Spirit as their guide.

"And I will ask the Father, and he will give you another advocate to help you and be with you forever— the Spirit of truth. The world cannot accept him, because it neither sees him nor knows him. But you know him, for he lives with you and will be in you." John 14:16-17.

"All this I have spoken while still with you. But the Advocate, the Holy Spirit, whom the Father will send in my name, will teach you all things and will remind you of everything I have said to you." John 14:25-26.

Once we accepted and believed in the saving power of Jesus Christ, we were given the gift of the Holy Spirit which became active through baptism of the Holy Spirit. We, as Christians, have this great privilege. The power of the Holy Spirit living within us is greater than the power of the world. As men and women living in our physical bodies, we are limited only by what our physical bodies can do. The work of the Holy Spirit is to enable us to move beyond the limits of our physical being and do feats like what Jesus did. This is the promise given by Jesus to His disciples and this promise still holds true for us in the present generation.

"Very truly I tell you, whoever believes in me will do the works I have been doing, and they will do even greater things than these, because I am going to the Father." John 14:12.

How comforting it is to know that we don't have to rely in our own strength and wisdom alone, especially when things get difficult and too hard to bear. What a privilege to have a friend who is only one call away and is available 24/7 to help and guide us. The Holy Spirit within us is just waiting for our call.

THE STORY OF DANIEL

The late seventh century B.C. was a time of great upheaval for the Jewish people. The Lord pronounced His divine judgment upon the nation of Israel for their idolatrous sins and their apathy towards His righteousness. For generations, the Lord was patient towards His people; but finally the society had become so corrupt, judgment was imminent. Still, among all the corruption and backsliding, there remained a few faithful and pure-hearted.

False prophets arose and proclaimed times of prosperity, yet God's favor cannot rest in a land without wholehearted repentance. The true prophets who fearlessly warned of impending judgment were ruthlessly tortured and imprisoned. Very few people wanted to turn from their wickedness. Those who were wise enough to heed the Words of the Lord from the prophets realized the nation was long over-due her time of punishment.

Babylon had conquered the Jewish people and at the time the Jewish people were taken into captivity, Daniel was just a young man. The King of Babylon ordered his soldiers to select only the finest, skilled men to assist in service in the king's palace. The Bible describes these selected Jews as being: "handsome in appearance, skillful in all wisdom, and cunning in knowledge and understanding of science"(Daniel 1:4). Since Daniel met these qualifications, by the fall of 605 B.C., as soldiers ransacked the Jewish homes throughout Judah, Daniel was torn from his family and familiar surroundings.

Without question, life in Babylon was a heart-stabbing shock for the young men of Judah. Remembering the times of the evening sacrifices in the temple at Jerusalem and rejoicing in the Lord's presence was still seared upon Daniel's memory. But now, in captivity, the Babylonians attempted to dissolve all the former memories of the life he'd known before. He was being assimilated into the Babylonian culture—a pagan civilization that the remnant of the God-fearing Jews detested.

The Babylonians sought to make the people of Israel completely forget their God, country, and religious practices. Upon arriving in Babylon, Daniel's name, which means "God is Judge" was immediately changed to the Babylonian name, "Belteshazzer" or 'Keeper of the hidden treasures of Bel'.

The communal aspect of prayer in the temple was unknown in Babylon. There were no religious leaders or rabbis to guide the people as before. The Torah wasn't openly taught, but rather suppressed. Where people once heard rejoicing and praise in the streets of Jerusalem, the captivity lead them to a land where pagan chants hovered over the city.

The Jews were required to adopt the Babylonian diet, and it would have been shocking for Daniel to see shellfish, pigs, and turtles incorporated into cuisine. It would be similar to us seeing a dinner with sautéed canine or stuffed vulture! These things were simply not regarded as food by the ancient Israelites. Even if they were given "clean" animals, none of the Babylonian slaughter practices would have been kosher; blood would have still filled the meat.

The common drink of the Babylonians was beer (which was often consumed on a daily basis). In addition to these things, the foods and drinks would have been dedicated to their gods and goddesses (1 Corinthians 10:28).

Now we have a better understanding why Daniel and his friends pleaded for the chief eunuch to give them only fruits, vegetables, pulses and water! The young men of Judah were familiar with the diet of their ancestors—filled with homegrown vegetables and fruits, barley, wheat, nuts, seeds, and kosher meats. For drink, they would have had lightly fermented wine, pure water, and perhaps fermented dairy products, such as kefir.

Daniel and his friends were in a dark place – a place that threatened their very identity, health, and relationship with the Lord. But they chose to take a stand and not corrupt themselves with the things common in that culture. They chose to set themselves apart—both physically and spiritually.

Do you notice parallels with the end-time world?

God loves us and He only wants the best for us. He is mindful of our well-being and is concerned with our lifestyle, especially in terms of what we eat.

Our body was given to us so that God would have a vessel on earth to carry out His Divine plans. Our body is the temple of the Holy Spirit, that's why we have to take care of it if we want God to have a clean and healthy dwelling place.

WHAT IS THE DANIEL FAST?

The "Daniel Fast" is a partial fast, based on a whole-food, plant-based diet practiced by Adam and Eve in the Garden of Eden. Today, some would refer to it as a vegan diet. The Daniel Fast is based upon the Old Testament prophet, Daniel, who intentionally and willingly abstains from certain foods for spiritual reasons. The first time Daniel fasts is in Daniel, Chapter 1:3-15.

The first time he fasted was for ten days. The purpose was more for the benefit of others than for himself. He knew the physical, mental, and spiritual benefits of his dietary habits. But the Babylonians did not—not until they saw for themselves the benefits of eating the foods God designed our bodies to optimally 'operate' on.

The second time Daniel fasted was to enable Daniel to hear God more clearly—to bring his body under the control of the spirit rather than the other way around (giving into cravings, eating for comfort, out of boredom, etc.). Both times, however, Daniel's fasting was for the glory of God. And that's what your fasting should be about, too. Fasting isn't a diet. Yes, your body benefits tremendously, but that's because in fasting you are giving your body back to God spiritually and physically. My prayer is that you will use each of the following twenty-one days to allow God to change you from the inside out—physically, emotionally, and spiritually.

PRAY: LORD, Thank you for Daniel's life and for sharing it with us in the Bible. Thank you for the example he presents. I've not faced anything like Daniel faced, so any excuse I thought I had for not putting you first or sharing the truth of the Gospel is nothing. Let me use this time of fasting to become bolder for the name of Jesus. In Jesus' name I pray, Amen.

PREPARING FOR THE 21 DAY DANIEL FAST

A very important part of the fast is to properly plan for the fast. Fasting is an act of humility and consecration,

"I put on sackcloth and humbled myself with fasting."(Psalm 35:13)

Since fasting is a spiritual practice, it is crucial for us to have an intimate relationship with God. Humbling ourselves in prayer, we have instant admission to the heart of God. Fasting requires faith, prayer and commitment. Without these three, your fast would become merely a period of changing your eating habits. Before you begin your fast, remind yourself of how big God is. Remember all His attributes.

Keep in mind that God has big plans for you and that He wants to partner with you. Doing this will strengthen your faith and will solidify your commitment to Him throughout the fast.

PREPARE YOUR BODY BEFORE THE FAST

Consult your healthcare professional about any medications you may be using. As you lose weight and detoxify, your medications may have to be adjusted accordingly. Weigh yourself, write it down and take a photo when you start so that you have a record of your starting point.

Two to four days before beginning the fast, it is advisable to eliminate caffeine, refined sugar, alcohol, tobacco, refined foods, fast foods, restaurant food, MSG, GMO, white flour, fried food, boxed dinners, processed meats, shellfish (e.g., crab, lobster, shrimp), pork.

Withdrawal from caffeine, sugar and additives may cause symptoms. You might experience headaches, shakiness, bloating, constipation or diarrhea. The pre-fasting phase should take between 2-3 days. Slowly increase your fiber and water intake as well. It is good to start eating more fruits and vegetables before you begin your fast. Start the day with 1 glass (8 oz.) of lemon water. Squeeze ½ lemon into 8 oz. of fresh, filtered water and drink. Allow 15 minutes before drinking or eating. Buy organic fruit and vegetables if possible. Make sure to drink plenty (6-8 glasses per day) of fresh clean water to eliminate and flush away toxins. Become an avid reader of all nutrition labels. You will be surprised how much you will learn about hidden ingredients, nutrition, vitamins, minerals and calories. Institute a consistent exercise routine (swimming, walking, running, hiking, biking, weight lifting, stretching). If you find yourself having a weak moment, immediately say a prayer of strength.

DURING THE FAST

The 21- Daniel Fast is a partial fast which means that you will trim down several foods from your diet and focus on eating fruits, vegetables and pulses (seeds, nuts, and legumes). During this phase, you will also concentrate on prayer. As part of your fast, you are going to eat and drink only foods that are permitted from the Daniel Fast List. You may refer to the 21 Day Daniel Fast Prayer and Toolbox for the list of foods to eat and avoid. Please print the list and take it with you when you shop every week. The good thing about planning your meals is that you won't have to think so much about what you are going to eat. Many have failed in achieving their spiritual goals in fasting just because they were too concerned about what they were going to eat. They spent a huge amount of time in planning their meals instead of praying and meditating on God's Word. You don't want that to happen to you. So before you begin your fast, make sure that you have at least a few breakfast, lunch, and dinner options. (See 21 Day Daniel Fast Prayer and Toolbox for the list of recipes and meal ideas). As you can see in the sample menu ideas, you have a lot of options available. Make sure you drink a lot of water, walk every day and rest as much as your schedule will allow. As you continue to fast, you will likely experience amazing transformation both physically and spiritually.

However, the most important thing above all is to have a heart that seeks to glorify God. Fasting for health purposes is one thing. But fasting for spiritual purposes is the true essence of fasting.

The Bible says, "Whether you eat or drink or whatever you do, do it all for the glory of God." - 1 Corinthians 10:31.

HERE ARE SOME SUGGESTIONS AND TIPS

Eat fresh foods fruits, vegetables, seeds, nuts, beans, legumes and pulses made as homemade soups, stews, fresh smoothies and homemade juices (using a juicer at home, not store bought juices) with an approximate ratio of 20% fresh fruits and 80% fresh vegetables. It is recommended to use fresh, organic produce due to the abundance of pesticides that reside within most conventional, as well as the higher content of antioxidants within organic. Do not use only fruit juices because of the high sugar content and lack of fiber from juicing. When we juice, we are only getting the nutrients within the fruit and not the benefits of fiber, therefore it will spike our blood sugar immensely. By making sure you are only using 20% fruit and 80% vegetables, this will allow your blood sugar to level out more evenly from the other nutrients you are getting within the vegetables. The fruits are used to sweeten the juice and give a pleasant taste. If the juice tastes too strong, you can dilute it with water.

Before you use legumes and beans, it is advisable to soak them in water overnight to avoid bloating and possible indigestion. You can soak seeds and nuts for 1 hour, drain and use. Fruits and vegetables should be washed thoroughly.

PREPARE YOURSELF EMOTIONALLY & MENTALLY

Prepare yourself for temporary emotional and mental discomforts, such as impatience, irritation and anxiety. Due to a changed diet, you may experience some headaches, fatigue and sleeplessness. When you are psychologically prepared for this, you will not be distracted from your schedule. The first two or three days are usually the hardest. As you continue to fast, you will experience a sense of well-being.

PREPARE YOURSELF SPIRITUALLY

Fasting is a time for prayer, and lots of prayer. Daniel had a specific time and place for prayer. He prayed three times a day in his room, with windows open facing Jerusalem. This season of fasting gives us an opportunity to humble ourselves before God and to be more diligent in seeking Him and His revelations.

Be aware that you will encounter spiritual resistance. Satan does not want you to enhance your relationship with God and he may try to derail your mission. Here are some signs that you may be under spiritual attack.
• Struggling with overwhelming feelings of discouragement.
• Loss of sleep due to unnecessary interruptions and nightmares.
• Struggling with doubts, fear and unnecessary worries.
• Overwhelming sense of condemnation over sins you
  have previously overcome.
• Crippling temptations that you find difficult to resist.
• Unending pressure in important relationships.
• Unnecessary confusion.

IF YOU RECOGNIZE ANY OF THESE SIGNS MANIFESTING, DECLARE YOUR POWER OVER THEM USING THE WORD OF GOD. PRAY FOR PROTECTION AND DELIVERANCE.

SET A CLEAR VISION FOR YOUR FAST.
WHY AM I FASTING?

Think of the things that you want to pray for. What motivated you to pursue this fast? Is there a specific objective in entering this fast? Are you praying for healing? Salvation of a loved one? Reconciliation? Spiritual Growth? Breaking strongholds? It is important to have a specific objective or purpose for your fast so that you will have a specific direction and prayer focus. Make a list of all your prayer points. Writing down your prayer points will help you stay committed to your fast. During your fast, you will receive revelations pertaining to certain things. When you don't know what you are praying for, there is a huge chance that those revelations will go to waste. It's like having lots of arrows but having no target board to shoot them into. Having a clear vision will help you to become more determined. Daniel's vision upon entering the palace and engaging in a ten-day fast was for him to be used mightily by God. Setting a clear purpose for your fast will give you the strength to overcome temptations because you are focused on your goals.

CHOOSE YOUR FASTING PRAYER PARTNERS.
JOIN OR START A FASTING GROUP

Have a buddy system. Most people find they do better when they aren't alone in this time of fasting and Bible study. Daniel wasn't alone during his first time, either, you know. He had Shadrach, Meshach, and Abednego as fasting partners. Not only will your prayer/fasting partners serve as a source of encouragement and accountability, they will also be those you can share your heart with. Resist the temptation to lecture, council or judge each other. One of the most important points is to keep all information within the group confidential in order to create a secure environment of trust for all. You should also meet regularly and ask for help anytime you need it.

Involve your Family or/and Friends or/and Neighbors and co-workers.

"Therefore, confess your sins to one another and pray for one another, that you may be healed'. - James 5:16.
"If we confess our sins, he is faithful and just and will forgive us our sins and purify us from all unrighteousness". - 1 John 1:9.
"Carry each other's burdens, and in this way you will fulfill the law of Christ". - Galatians 6:2.

MAKE A COMMITMENT

It is important to know when to start and end your fast so that you can prepare properly and stick to the schedule. A Daniel Fast is usually done for twenty-one consecutive days. The start of the fast takes place on sunrise of the first day and ends on sundown of the last day. You should create 2 schedules. One for your spiritual routine and one for your physical routine. Get with your partners and decide what prayer topics, devotionals, prayer needs and Bible books you will be focusing on. Also, make sure you have the proper foods available for the week's meals. If you are planning to abstain from social media or any form of communication throughout the duration of the fast, you might want to inform your friends and family about the schedule of your fast so that they will know how and where to reach you.

SPENDING TIME IN GOD'S WORD - JOURNAL AND ALLOWING GOD TO SPEAK TO YOU!

Just like prayer and fasting, reading your Bible is about bonding to God in a more powerful way. As you set aside time to seek God through your devotional time, you will experience His presence and hear his voice. While you are reading your daily passage, identify a scripture verse from the passage that stands out to you. Write it out in full in you journal and allow God to speak as you write.

Ask the Holy Spirit to show you what God is saying. How does this apply to your life right now? Thank God for revealing His truths to you. Remember, prayer is a two- way conversation, so listen for what God wants to say to you.

SUGGESTED BIBLE STUDY METHODS:

Soak Method :

- **SCRIPTURE** – read the selected scripture.
- **OBSERVATION** – what stands out to you in the scripture?
- **APPLICATION** – how can you apply it in your life?
- **KNEEL** – kneel and pray about it.

Power Method :

- **PRAY** – begin with prayer.
- **OBSERVE** – what is the lesson of the scripture?
- **WRITE** – transcribe any thoughts that stand out to you.
- **ENVISION** – imagine how it applies in your life.
- **RESPOND** – respond to any instructions.

ESTABLISH A DEFINITE PRAYER TIME

If you want your spirit to be as healthy as your body, you have to make sure to feed it as much as you feed your body. Wake up an hour early and set aside that hour for Morning Prayer. If your schedule does not permit, you can have your prayer time during your morning drive or morning commute. In the afternoon, if you are working, you can divide your lunch hour. Set aside 30 minutes for eating and the other 30 minutes for prayer. The best time to pray at night is right before you go to sleep. Set aside a few minutes or an hour for Bible reading and prayer. This will also help you reflect on all the things that happened throughout the day and all the blessings that you have received.

CHOOSE A DEFINITE PLACE FOR PRAYER

Choose a quiet place for prayer and meditation. It can be in the following places:
- In your room
- In your car (during your drive to or from work)
- Inside your office cubicle during lunch hour
- In the park (if you have time on weekdays)
- Anywhere that is convenient for you

BECOME A PRAYER WARRIOR.
PRAYING ACCORDING TO GOD'S WORD

Now that you have prepared yourself for the fast and have set-up a dietary plan, let us now talk about another important factor that would make your prayer and fasting experience a powerful and effective one. When I was a new Christian, I didn't know how to pray. I understood that prayer was a communication between me and God. Yes, I talked to God but I didn't know how He would answer. I thought that God's response should always be favorable and that it should only come in a form of obvious answers like receiving a money miracle when I ask for provision, or passing a test when I have prayed that I would. As I prayed a lot of prayers, I went through a time when I almost gave up praying because most of my prayers went unanswered. I had a problem with accepting the fact that almost always, I didn't get what I wanted.

IS IT ABOUT WHAT YOU WANT OR WHAT HE WANTS?

"You do not have because you do not ask God. When you ask, you do not receive, because you ask with wrong motives, that you may spend what you get on your pleasures." James 4:2-3.
Sometimes, when we pray, we ask for a lot of petitions that focus on our own desires. There is nothing wrong with bringing our desires to the throne. God actually wants that because He is very much delighted with the prayers of His people. The only problem is when those desires were fueled by selfish motives.

God is not a selfish God. In fact, He is a generous God, and He only wants the best for us. God wants to say yes to your prayers as much as possible. We are His children and He wants to lavish us with His gifts. However, He is more concerned with our character than our comfort. As much as He wanted to say yes to some of our requests, He couldn't, because He knows that we will come to ruin once our self-centered desires are gratified.

That's why it is very important to open our hearts to God before we begin our fast. Allowing God to examine our hearts and to filter all our personal desires based on His holy purposes will enable us to turn our focus from ourselves to Him. Once we have conditioned ourselves into thinking about what God wants instead of what we want, then we are one step closer to achieving our breakthroughs.

SUGGESTED PRAYER METHODS:

Here are a few prayer methods to help keep you focused during your prayer time.

ACTS Prayer Method

- **ADORATION** - worship and glorifying God
- **CONFESSION** – confess our sins
- **THANKSGIVING** – thank God for all he has done for us
- **SUPPLICATION** – pray for others

PRAY Prayer Method

- **PRAISE** – praise him for who he is
- **REPENT** – admit your sins
- **ASK** – prayer requests
- **YIELD** – stop and listen to God

SHOW ME YOUR WILL LORD

Turning our focus from ourselves towards God requires patience and discipline. It doesn't just happen overnight. Before we met God, we used to make decisions on our own; we used to be ruled by our own will, we did things our own way and we had no problem with responding to our own fleshly desires. When God came into our lives, we were asked to humbly submit to His great authority. Doing so meant sacrificing our own will by doing things His way. We were asked to abandon the flesh and operate in the spirit instead. We no longer make our decisions on our own because we now consider what God has to say.

I remember crossing the street in a foreign country. I always looked at the wrong direction because I was used to following the traffic rules in my home country where drivers drive on the right. I was always looking on the left when I was supposed to be anticipating cars to come from right and vice versa. I almost got hit by a car because I was looking on the wrong side. It took me several days before I got used to that flow of traffic and be able to cross the road smoothly. It's the same way with our relationship with God, there were times when we still go back to our wrong patterns of thinking just because our minds were conditioned to think that way. This is the importance of constantly subjecting our thoughts and desires to God's will and plan for our lives – to make sure that we are looking on the right direction. One way to know God's will is through the Scriptures. There are a lot of promises, decrees, and commands in the Bible. God has given those promises and imposed those laws for a purpose – it is for us to live our Christian lives to the fullest; to be used mightily by God while enjoying His precious gifts to us.

If we want to pray for things that are sure to be answered, then we have to pray according to God's will. When we pray according to God's promises in the Bible, our prayers will not go in vain because God never breaks His promises. Jesus was able to persevere in His fasting because God's will was clear to Him. He knew the end of the matter and He knew that He would be victorious. Every time He was tempted by the devil, He always responded by saying "It is written..." God's Word is like a gushing spring where we can always draw water from whenever we feel thirsty for hope. It is overflowing and the answers we are looking for are crystal clear.

HOW TO BREAK YOUR FAST

Congratulations, you made it! You have a new body that is clean, detoxified and light. Breaking your fast gradually is extremely important for your health. Now you can add smoothies, simple vegetable soups, and steamed vegetables for the first two days. After that, you can slowly transition back to a wholesome, healthy diet.

BACK TO HEALTHY YOU

Now that you are feeling the physical benefits of your transition, dedication, and hard work you should stick to a healthy, balanced diet. In order to strengthen your immune system, your diet should be a whole-food, plant-based, nutritionally-dense diet consisting mainly of fresh fruits and vegetables, legumes, probiotics, gluten free grains, nuts and seeds. It can also include very small amounts of meat that consists of free-range, organic poultry and wild-caught fish (no more than 6 oz. per week). During the colder months, you may need a little more meat and that's okay.

If you find any foods that cause a reaction, avoid them completely. You should exclude all canned, boxed, refined and processed foods. This will ensure that your body gets nutritionally dense foods without all of the harmful fats, salts and refined sugars.

Following a healthy, balanced plant-based diet along with regular fasting will ensure a wide array of health benefits, as well as prevention of some major diseases that seem to affect North America more so than other countries.

FREQUENTLY ASKED QUESTIONS

What makes "The Daniel Fast" different than other fasts?
What really makes it different than other fasts is that we look at more than just food and fitness. We integrate three additional components; the component of faith, which is the foundation; the component of friends, which is the context; and the component of focus, which is the direction and purpose. The Daniel Fast involves your mind, your spirit, your soul and your body – getting all these elements working together provides a way to make the long-lasting changes we all desire.

What about prepared foods?
Read the labels of all prepared foods. Remember the Daniel Fast is sugar free and chemical free. That is why I suggest organic, fresh or frozen foods.

What about pasta?
Make sure the label says whole grain or vegetable-based pasta like quinoa, black bean or brown rice with no additives, gluten, yeast or sugar. But, the diet should consist mostly of vegetables and fruits.

What about roasted nuts?
Try to stick to organic, raw, unsalted nuts and/or soaked or sprouted ones. These are harder to find, so if you have to choose roasted nuts, then get plain roasted, unsalted nuts with no preservatives.

How do I get enough protein in my diet while on the fast?
Protein-rich foods allowed on the Daniel Fast are almonds, sunflower seeds, lentils, quinoa, brown rice, split peas and some whole grains. Be sure you eat plenty of those.

What about salad dressing?
Salads are great on the Daniel Fast. Use olive oil and lemon or lime as salad dressing options.

Do I need to eat organic foods while on the fast?
You don't have to eat organic, but it is recommended because choosing them keeps toxins out of your foods, meaning no use of chemically formulated fertilizers, growth stimulants, antibiotics or pesticides.

Can I go out to eat?
Yes, you can. Just make sure what you get is compliant with the Daniel Fast, such as a salad with olive oil and a baked potato with no extras on it.

How much can I eat?
As long as your food choices fit the Daniel Fast, then you can eat all and as often as you want until you are satisfied!

What about bread?
No bread.

What if I want to do the Daniel Fast for dietary reasons and not spiritual purposes?
The definition of fasting is to restrict food for a spiritual purpose. Using the Daniel Fast eating plan for strictly health purposes would be a Daniel Diet rather than a fast. Many people do use the Daniel Fast eating plan to improve their health and for weight loss.

Can I take my medications?
While you are on the fast, you must consult with your doctor. Your dose may need to be adjusted.

Is it okay to take multivitamins and/or drink supplements?
No. Most supplements have fillers that would not be compatible with the diet.

Am I supposed to eat 3 times a day?
There is no mention about how often to eat in the Daniel Fast.

How can I identify whole grain products?
Whole grain products can be identified by the ingredient list. Typically if the ingredient lists "whole wheat", "rolled oats", or "whole corn" as the first ingredient, the product is a whole grain food item. Another way to identify whole grains in the foods you eat is to look in the nutritional facts information and check if the food item contains dietary fiber. If it contains a significant amount, it most likely contains whole grains. "Wheat flour" is not a whole grain and therefore does not indicate a whole grain product. Many breads are colored brown (often with molasses) and made to look like whole grain, but are not. Additionally, some food manufacturers make foods with whole grain ingredients, but because whole grain ingredients are not the dominant ingredient, they are not whole grain products.

What are pulses?
Some Bible translations used the term 'vegetables' instead of 'pulse'. But when we consider doing the Daniel fast, there are lots of food included in the list aside from vegetables. The Hebrew word of Pulse is zero-im (זרעים zēroîym) which refers to seeds of any kind – from the term zerua (זרע zâra), which means to disperse, to scatter seed, to sow. Pulse refers to any edible seed that grows in a pod. Pulses include all beans, peas and lentils, such as: baked beans, red, green, yellow and brown lentils, black-eyed peas, garden peas, runner beans, chickpeas, broad beans, kidney beans, and butter beans. Pulses are a great source of protein that can be a great alternative for meat, fish, and dairy products.

What are Kosher Foods?
In the Old Testament, there are strict Jewish dietary laws which is termed as kashrut in Hebrew. Kosher foods are ones that conform to the regulations of Kashrut. The Jewish Dietary Laws strictly comply with the dietary guidelines in Leviticus and Deuteronomy written in the Torah. Back in Moses' Day, God gave instructions to his people through Moses regarding the types of meat and other foods that are fit and unfit for consumption. The Law of Moses prohibits eating the meat of ceremonially unclean animals that would cause defilement to the body (see Leviticus 11). Daniel was aware of this and was determined to stick to God's Law. He was aware that the royal officials were not familiar with the Jewish dietary laws. Therefore, to make sure that he would not be defiled in any way, he resolved in drinking only water and eating pulses in place of meat (see Genesis 1:29).

What Are the Categories of Fasting Methods?

There are many different types of fasting. People choose different methods depending on their goals and comfort levels. Let's take a look at some of the most common approaches.

Supernatural "Divine" Fast:

By definition, a supernatural fast is going without any food or water for 40 days. Jesus, Moses, Elijah, and Joshua each fasted for 40 days. Deuteronomy 9:9-18, 1 Kings 19:4-8. Matthew 4:1-2.

Absolute Fast:

By definition, an absolute fast is going without any food or water for 24 or more hours.

This fast can be used in an emergency situation "life or death situations."

- 24 hr. Yom Kippur, also known as the Day of Atonement. Leviticus 23:27.
- 3-days. Esther fasted for the safety of the Jews – Esther 4:15-17.
- 3-days. Jonah's warning to Nineveh. Jonah 3:5.
- 3 days. Paul fasted after his conversion – Acts 9:1-9.
- 3 days. Ezra fasted while mourning over sin – Ezra 10:6-17.
- 7 days. David mourning his child's illness – 2 Samuel 12:1-23.
- 1 day. Darius fasted for the safety of Daniel – Daniel 6:18-23.

24-Hour Water Fast "Sundown to Sundown":

You fast for a full 24 hours, you don't eat anything for a full 24 hours. You may drink only water.

Liquid Fast:

A liquid fast is essentially abstaining from all solid food, but you may have some liquids other than water. There are different variations to liquid fasts. Depending on the method chosen, you may have clear liquids, or substantial liquids such as juices, broths, or smoothies. A few examples include:

- **Water-only fast**: Consuming nothing but water for an extended period.

- **Juice Fast**: Consumption of juiced vegetables and fruits only. This would not include any pulp or fiber of any kind, just the clear liquids from juicing vegetables or fruits.

- **Green Smoothie Fast**: A green smoothie fast will have the most calories and nutrient density of the liquid fasting options. In this type of fast, you can blend any combination of fruits and vegetables you like in a blender. Blending will give you the most nutrients (vitamins, minerals, and phytonutrients) along with fiber. This is the most 'satiating' of the liquid fast options.

Partial fasting- Daniel Fast:

As with liquid fasts, there are several variations to partial fasting. All partial fasts include some addition of solid food but minimizes certain foods to relieve the body of excessive digestive burden.

Examples of partial fasts include the 10 - 21 Day Daniel Fast.

What is the Difference between Fasting and Intermittent Fasting?
Fasting is abstinence from all food or drink for a specific period of time. In the Bible, there are records of fasts of differing lengths, from 24 hours to 40 days. On the other hand, Intermittent Fasting (IF) is abstinence from certain foods or drinks for a specific period of time. Intermittent fasting is not a diet but rather an eating pattern. It splits a day into periods of eating and fasting, which you alternate. Everyone fasts nightly during time of sleep. That is called the fasting time. During the daytime, we all eat. That is called the eating time. Daniel Fast is not an InTermittent Fast, however, you can incorporate intermittent fasting methods into the Daniel Fast by skipping a meal our using other ideas below.

What are the Intermittent Fasting Methods?
There are several different methods to IF; they range from simply delaying your breakfast, to fasting for a full 24 hours. Let's take a look at several options.

Meal Skipping
There are really no rules to this method. You simply skip a meal intentionally whenever you feel like it. This can be the easiest method because you get to choose when it works for you. If you have an excessively active day or have dinner plans, meal skipping may not be practical.

16/8 Method or "Skipping a Breakfast"
You are shortening your 'feeding window' to only 8 hours. For most people, this means not eating breakfast, and only consuming two meals per day. For example: eat your first meal at 12 noon, eat dinner at 7 pm, and take your last bite of food by 8 pm. Don't consume any calories until 12 noon the next day. You can do this fasting Method 1-4 times per week.

20/4 Method = O.M.A.D (one meal a day)
This method can be a little trickier for some, but many people find they enjoy the freedom of not having to think about food except one time per day. In the 20/4 method, your 'feeding window' is only four hours. For most people, this means eating one substantial meal per day. The timing depends on your schedule and preference, but many people choose to have a large dinner. As an example, you can begin eating at 4 pm and finish all caloric intake by 8 pm. This allows for a nice casual dinner, allows you to slow down, enjoy your food, have conversations with friends, and be mindful of your eating practices. You can do this fasting method 1-3 times per week.

How to incorporate Daniel Fast into other methods of fasting?
This will be determined by your fasting experience and your health status. You can incorporate any fasting method as long as you stay within the protocol. For example, you can choose 1 day solid food and 1 day liquid or 24 hour water fast. For beginners, you may want to choose to skip a meal, 16/8 Method or one meal a day method (OMAD).

What happens to your body when you fast?

To understand how fasting works, let's have a brief primer on metabolism. The human body uses glucose as its primary energy source. It depends on a steady(ish) supply over the course of the day to meet its energy demands. The body will store glucose in the liver and muscle cells to use throughout the day and in-between meal times. If the body is not fed for an extended time, stored glucose (glycogen) will become depleted. This usually happens between 12-16 hours depending on physical activity levels and the metabolic health of the person. It's during this time that autophagy happens. Autophagy is the bodies' way to clean up cellular debris. This process enables the body to regulate the health of the cell and get rid of toxic waste products and pathogens.

The benefits of autophagy include:
1. Neuroprotective benefits
2. Increased life span
3. Helps modulate rogue cell growth
4. Enhances immunity and modulates inflammation

When glycogen stores are depleted, the body must use an alternate form of fuel, namely, amino acids and fatty acids. This is a process called gluconeogenesis. Eventually, these reserves become depleted as well, and the body will enter ketosis or the process of using ketone bodies for fuel. The conversion into ketosis usually takes about two days for most people, though it can take up to a week from some. While the conversion of burning glucose to burning ketones can be very uncomfortable, most people report an increased feeling of energy, mental clarity, improved sleep, improved endurance, and stable blood sugar once they are in ketosis. The scientific research surrounding ketosis has shown an improvement in inflammation modulation, weight loss, blood sugar stabilization, improved mitochondrial function, and substantial anecdotal reports of improved health and vitality.

Longer fasts consisting of a week or several weeks, are lacking in significant scientific research since most medical professions consider it dangerous, and it would not be considered ethical to conduct such studies. There have been a few cases where longer fasts were medically supervised, and have shown interesting results. In one study, it was found that longer fasts (around 10 days) showed benefits for cardiovascular health and hypertension. In another infamous case, a man underwent 382 days of medically supervised fasting. He lost 276 pounds and improved his blood sugar markers. He purportedly suffered no ill health effects. Outside of a few other reports of week or month long fasting, the scientific literature has very little documentation on extended fasting.

What are Some of the Benefits of Intermittent Fasting?

1. Reduced risk of chronic health conditions
2. Can reduce insulin resistance, lowering your risk of type 2 diabetes
3. Beneficial for heart health
4. Can reduce oxidative stress and inflammation in the body
5. Good for your brain: improved mental concentration, sharpness and clarity
6. Improvement in hormone profile
7. Cleaning of waste cells and pathogens
8. May help prevent & protects against neurodegenerative diseases such as Alzheimer's & Parkinson's
9. Allows the GI tract to rest and repair
10. Helps promote deep sleep.
11. Reduces inflammation and physical stress
12. Normalize insulin imbalance
13. Lowers bad cholesterol.
14. Weight management
15. Increased longevity
16. May enhanced stem cell production
17. DNA repairer

TESTIMONIALS

God's Grace is Sufficient

I was going through a very difficult emotional time with 2 serious illnesses in my family. I was concerned about my son who was 48 years old, father of 3, with Parkinson's disease symptoms (trouble walking, talking and was completely disabled). Doctors prescribed many different medications that weren't working and he was running out of options. Also, my grandson, who was 17 was having to undergo complete large intestine resection (removal). I had decided that I wanted to spend more time in prayer and this would be an excellent time to do the Daniel Fast and prayer with Maria. I hoped to gain mental, emotional, spiritual and health benefits – which I did.

In the beginning, I wasn't sure if I could do it. I was 78 years old, was ill myself with polycyhtemia vera (blood cancer), and wasn't sure that I could go 21 days with the dietary restrictions that the Daniel Fast required. Giving up meat and white flour was no problem, it was the coffee that I was addicted to. How would I function without my 3 cups of coffee in the morning? I prayed for a more positive attitude about the whole thing, cleaned out my refrigerator and cupboards and went shopping with the Daniel Fast shopping list. Once I eliminated flour, sugar and meat from my diet and began having fresh juices and vegetables, I began to realize how much better I felt. As each day passed, I began to feel better and better. My body seemed to respond positively to this style of eating. I no longer had cravings for sugar products (sweets), fatty fried foods, pancakes, pasta, etc. Instead I learned how to substitute my diet with healthier alternatives that were allowed. I never felt hungry.

Each day I began with devotions and prayer for the health of my family and my own, asking God to give me discernment on what I could and couldn't change, As I read the Scriptures, it seemed that I was being fed with God's word exactly what I needed. I felt a calmness come over me as I put my trust in the Lord.

Miraculously, my son was chosen for a new medical procedure which has helped him greatly and my grandson came through his surgery ordeal with flying colors. Not only did I feel healthier and have my prayers answered after the fast, I also lost 10 lbs. Would I recommend the Daniel Fast to others? Yes. I am about to start the Daniel Fast again, eliminating sugar, fried foods, flour, meat, bread, etc. one week before starting the fast as a process of cleansing to become ready for the fast. For me, it is not a time of sacrifice, but a time to draw closer to God and hear his voice. Yes, it requires planning and a little more preparation, but it helps you to realize why you are doing it and what is really important in life. I never did go back to my old way of eating and I feel much better now. I know this time will benefit me even more. It gets easier each time I do the Daniel Fast. I wish you much success in your Daniel Fast.
– Mary C.

Heartbroken Mother Prays for Her Homeless Addict Sons

Each time that I do the Daniel Fast, I ask the Lord to provide a partner for me. He has never failed, and the partners have often come in unexpected and unusual ways.

Julie was a woman that had I worked with several years earlier but I had not seen her for about 5 years. Julie and I saw each other at a mutual friend's house and she commented that I had lost weight. She asked, "How did you lose weight?" I told her that I was praying and fasting, not for weight loss, but for spiritual breakthrough. I told her I was preparing for a Daniel Fast and to my surprise she said, "Can I do it with you?" Of course I said yes. She also confided in me that her twin sons, aged about 20, were both addicted to drugs and were both in very bad shape and she wanted to pray and fast for them. She said that her sons had gotten jobs at the casino making a lot of cash and soon they both became heavily involved in drugs and became addicted. They had both attempted to recover through various programs but had not been successful. They were still addicted and sinking fast.

Julie was not even a follower of Christ at that time. I told her that in order for us to pray and fast together, we needed to be on the same page. We should be praying in the name of Jesus and she needed to be "born again". I explained that we would be lead by the spirit and she needs to have the Holy Spirit inside her. I asked if she would like to accept Jesus as her savior and she said yes! We then started sharing our hearts and burdens to each other. We had a wonderful time enjoying eachother's company during the Daniel Fast and grew closer together and closer to God.

About 6 months after we fasted together, one of her sons started to clean up and he was successful in kicking the drugs but the other one was in bad shape. Julie found her son on the street, homeless. She brought him home and fed him and took care of him. The next day, she came home to find him on the floor unconscious and she decided to yell to God for help. In the next few months, God's work become apparent in their lives. He met an old friend who asked him to attend a church function. It was there that he realized what was missing in his life, Jesus. He quit the drugs and began attending church. He then accepted Jesus as his savior! Both her sons are now active members in their local Christian church. **Wow!**

Sometimes we need to be broken before God can put us back together again, properly.

Suicidal Jewish Doctor Finds Jesus

I had been looking for a general practitioner for some time when I was referred by a friend to Dr. Bloom. Dr. Bloom was a wonderful doctor who had a genuine concern for me. I could feel it. Whenever I was in her office, I felt like I was her number one concern. She spent time with me, asked good questions and took as much time as she needed, sometimes an hour to get to the root of a problem. We also became good friends and she would invite me to her home and I invited her to mine. We lost contact for a while as I became a snowbird and would go to Florida for the winters.

My birthday is in the summer and I invited her, via text message, to my birthday party. To my surprise and delight she showed up. She seemed a little down so I asked her what was wrong. She then told me her story. She had met a man, a doctor who was 15 years older than her, and they were living together in his house. She had sold all her furniture and moved in with him. He had some health issues and she nursed him back to health. After he regained his health, everything went well for a time. Then she found out that he was cheating on her and he kicked her out of his house. Around the same time, her secretary failed to file some required paperwork and she ended up losing her license and her medical practice. She was so depressed that she attempted suicide by injecting herself with a lethal dose of insulin. Her neighbor found her lying on her floor and called the ambulance. Miraculously, she recovered. She was obviously brokenhearted.

She asked me to go to dinner and I told her that I was planning to do a fast and prayer. She immediately said, "I would like to join you and can we include Yom Kippur into the fast?" (Yom Kippur was a few days away and she was Jewish.) My doctor did not know about Jesus or even that Jesus was Jewish. I asked her if she would like to know more about Jesus and she said that a collegue she used to work with at the hospital had been inviting her to a Christian Bible Study for nearly 20 years, but she always declined to go. I told her that I would go with her if she wanted to go, and she agreed. When we arrived, she saw her friend from the hospital there and she felt comfortable. After the Bible study, we were introduced to the Bible teacher and chatted for a while. When the Bible teacher (pastor) asked her what is stopping her from accepting Jesus as her savior, she replied, "I do not like to betray my Jewish God and my people. There was a long silence and no one said anything. I could see the strong emotions overtaking her body. The Holy Spirit was melting her heart. With a trembling voice she then said, "Now I realize that Jesus was Jewish and he is the promised Messiah and He saved me!" She then accepted Jesus as her savior. She said she felt as if a huge weight was lifted from her shoulders. She felt free at last.

Salvation is a miracle! I was so grateful to be able to witness these amazing transformations of salvation, healing and deliverance. My prayer is that your testimonial will be an encouragement to someone else.

A Final Word

If you sincerely humble yourself before the Lord, repent, pray, and seek God's face; if you consistently meditate on His Word, you will experience a heightened awareness of His presence (John 14:21). The Lord will give you fresh, new spiritual insights. Your confidence and faith in God will be strengthened. You will feel mentally, spiritually, and physically refreshed. You will see answers to your prayers.

A single fast, however, is not a spiritual cure-all. Just as we need fresh infillings of the Holy Spirit daily, we also need new times of fasting before God. The Daniel Fast has been greatly rewarding to many Christians.

I encourage you to join me in fasting and prayer again and again until we truly experience revival in our homes, our churches, our beloved nation, and throughout the world.

 A. B. C. D. OF SALVATION

------------------------ SAVE ME, O LORD ------------------------

 ACCEPT YOU ARE SINNER

"For all have sinned and fall short of the glory of God." Romans 3:23.

"For the wages of sin is death, but the free gift of God is eternal life in Christ Jesus our Lord." Romans 6:23.

If we confess our sins, he is faithful and just and will forgive us our sins and purify us from all unrighteousness". 1 John 1:9.

 BELIVE JESUS CHRIST IS YOUR SAVIOR AND THE SON OF GOD.

Jesus said to him, "I am the way, and the truth, and the life. No one comes to the Father except through me." John 14:6.

"For God so loved the world, that he gave his only Son, that whoever believes in him should not perish but have eternal life." John 3:16.

 CONFESS & REPENT WITH YOUR MOUTH THAT JESUS IS LORD

"Because, if you confess with your mouth that Jesus is Lord and believe in your heart that God raised him from the dead, you will be saved." Romans 10:9

"For with the heart one believes and is justified, and with the mouth one confesses and is saved". Romans 10:10

"For by grace you have been saved through faith. And this is not your own doing; it is the gift of God, not a result of works, so that no one may boast." Ephesians 2:8-9

 DECIDE TO BE BAPTIZED "YOU MUST BE BORN AGAIN"

"Jesus answered, "Truly, truly, I say to you, unless one is born of water and the Spirit, he cannot enter the kingdom of God." John 3:5.

"And Peter said to them, "Repent and be baptized every one of you in the name of Jesus Christ for the forgiveness of your sins, and you will receive the gift of the Holy Spirit." Acts 2:38.

"Whoever believes and is baptized will be saved, but whoever does not believe will be condemned." Mark 16:16.

GOD'S PROMISES FOR YOU

A new heart also will I give you, and a new spirit will I put within you: and I will take away the stony heart out of your flesh, and I will give you a heart of flesh. Ezekiel 36:26.

For I know the plans I have for you, declares the Lord, plans for welfare and not for evil, to give you a future and a hope. Jeremiah 29:11.

The Helper, the Holy Spirit, whom the Father will send in my name, will teach you everything and make you remember all that I have told you. John 14:26.

Fruit of the Spirit is love, joy, peace, patience, kindness, goodness, faithfulness, gentleness, self-control; against such things there is no law. Galatians 5:22-23.

'I will never leave you nor forsake you'. Hebrews 13:5b.

I will be their God and **they will be my children**...Revelation 21:7b.

THE SINNER'S PRAYER (PRAYER OF SALVATION)

Here is an example of a prayer you can say to receive Jesus as your Savior.

Dear Lord Jesus,

I know that I am a sinner, and I ask for your forgiveness. I believe you died for my sins and rose from the dead. I turn from my sins and invite you to come into my heart and life. I want to trust and follow You as my Lord and Savior. In Your Name.

Amen.

"SEARCH ME, God, AND KNOW MY heart; TEST ME AND KNOW MY ANXIOUS THOUGHTS. SEE IF THERE IS ANY OFFENSIVE WAY in me, AND LEAD ME IN THE WAY EVERLASTING

Psalm 139:23-24

21 DAY DANIEL FAST
WEEK I

"Let us then approach God's throne of grace
with confidence, so that we may receive mercy
and find grace to help us in our time of need."

Hebrews 4:16

GET SPIRITUALY READY

PRAYER THEME AND BIBLE VERSE

BIBLE VERSES

DAY 1

DAY 2

DAY 3

DAY 4

DAY 5

DAY 6

DAY 7

PRAYER REQUEST   Write your prayer requests in the prayer request section.

MY GOALS FOR ......

BIBLE READING PLAN

BODY:

SOUL-MIND:

SPIRIT:

Get Physically Ready

MEAL PLAN IDEAS · DATE: _____ TO _____

SHOPPING LIST

DAY 1

DAY 2

DAY 3

DAY 4

TO DO

DAY 5

DAY 6

DAY 7

"CREATE IN ME A

Pure

heart,

O GOD,

AND RENEW A STEADFAST **SPIRIT** WITHIN

Me."

PSALM 51:10

SCRIPTURE / READING   DAY 1

WHAT IS GOD SAYING TO ME?

LORD TEACH ME TO

I AM GRATEFUL

LORD I NEED YOUR HELP

PRAYER FOR ME   PRAYER FOR OTHERS

BIBLE STUDY

BOOK: _____   **CHAPTER:** _____

THEME: _____   **DATE:** _____   DAY 1

_____
_____
_____
_____
_____
_____
_____
_____
_____
_____
_____
_____
_____
_____
_____
_____
_____
_____
_____
_____
_____
_____
_____
_____

GOD'S PROMISES
_____
_____
_____
_____
_____

"HEAL ME, *O Lord,* AND I WILL BE HEALED; SAVE ME AND I WILL BE SAVED, FOR YOU ARE THE ONE *I praise.*"

JEREMIAH 17:14

DEVOTIONAL

SCRIPTURE / READING

WHAT IS GOD SAYING TO ME?

LORD TEACH ME TO

I AM GRATEFUL

LORD I NEED YOUR HELP

PRAYER FOR ME

PRAYER FOR OTHERS

BIBLE STUDY

BOOK: _____   CHAPTER: _____

THEME: _____   DATE: _____   DAY 2

GOD'S PROMISES

THEREFORE CONFESS YOUR SINS TO EACH OTHER AND PRAY FOR EACH OTHER SO THAT YOU MAY BE HEALED. THE PRAYER OF A RIGHTEOUS PERSON IS POWERFUL AND EFFECTIVE.

JAMES 5:16

WHAT IS GOD SAYING TO ME?

LORD TEACH ME TO

I AM GRATEFUL

LORD I NEED YOUR HELP

PRAYER FOR ME

PRAYER FOR OTHERS

BIBLE STUDY

BOOK: _____   **CHAPTER:** _____

THEME: _____   **DATE:** _____   DAY 3

_____

_____

_____

_____

_____

_____

_____

_____

_____

_____

_____

_____

_____

_____

_____

_____

_____

_____

_____

_____

_____

_____

_____

GOD'S PROMISES

_____

_____

_____

_____

AND WHEN YOU STAND *Praying,*

IF YOU HOLD **ANYTHING AGAINST ANYONE, FORGIVE THEM, SO THAT YOUR**

Father

IN HEAVEN MAY FORGIVE

YOU BY

YOUR SINS.

MARK 11:25.

WHAT IS GOD SAYING TO ME?

LORD TEACH ME TO

I AM GRATEFUL

LORD I NEED YOUR HELP

PRAYER FOR ME

PRAYER FOR OTHERS

BOOK: _____ **CHAPTER:** _____

THEME: _____ **DATE:** _____ DAY 4

_____
_____
_____
_____
_____
_____
_____
_____
_____
_____
_____
_____
_____
_____
_____
_____
_____
_____
_____
_____
_____
_____
_____
_____
_____
_____

GOD'S PROMISES

_____
_____
_____
_____

"BUT TO YOU WHO ARE LISTENING I SAY: *Love* YOUR ENEMIES, *Do good* TO THOSE WHO HATE YOU, *Bless those* WHO CURSE YOU, *Pray* FOR THOSE WHO MISTREAT YOU."

Luke 6:27-28

SCRIPTURE / READING

WHAT IS GOD SAYING TO ME?

LORD TEACH ME TO

I AM GRATEFUL

LORD I NEED YOUR HELP

PRAYER FOR ME

PRAYER FOR OTHERS

BOOK: _____   **CHAPTER:** _____

THEME: _____   **DATE:** _____   **DAY 5**

_____
_____
_____
_____
_____
_____
_____
_____
_____
_____
_____
_____
_____
_____
_____
_____
_____
_____
_____
_____
_____
_____
_____
_____
_____

GOD'S PROMISES
_____
_____
_____
_____
_____

SO WATCH YOURSELVES.

"IF YOUR BROTHER

OR SISTER

SINS AGAINST YOU,

Rebuke them;

AND IF THEY REPENT,

forgive them.

EVEN IF THEY SIN

AGAINST YOU

SEVEN TIMES IN A DAY
AND SEVEN TIMES
COME BACK TO YOU
SAYING 'I REPENT,'

YOU MUST

Forgive them.

LUKE 17:3-4

DEVOTIONAL

SCRIPTURE / READING

WHAT IS GOD SAYING TO ME?

LORD TEACH ME TO

I AM GRATEFUL

LORD I NEED YOUR HELP

PRAYER FOR ME

PRAYER FOR OTHERS

BOOK: _____   **CHAPTER:** _____

THEME: _____   **DATE:** _____   **DAY 6**

_____

_____

_____

_____

_____

_____

_____

_____

_____

_____

_____

_____

_____

_____

_____

_____

_____

_____

_____

_____

_____

_____

_____

GOD'S PROMISES

_____

_____

_____

_____

"GET RID OF ALL BITTERNESS, RAGE AND ANGER, BRAWLING AND SLANDER, ALONG WITH EVERY FORM OF MALICE. BE KIND AND COMPASSIONATE TO ONE ANOTHER, *forgiving* EACH OTHER, JUST AS IN CHRIST GOD *Forgave* YOU".

EPHESIANS 4:31-32

DEVOTIONAL

SCRIPTURE / READING

WHAT IS GOD SAYING TO ME?

LORD TEACH ME TO

I AM GRATEFUL

LORD I NEED YOUR HELP

PRAYER FOR ME

PRAYER FOR OTHERS

BIBLE STUDY

BOOK: _____   **CHAPTER:** _____

THEME: _____   **DATE:** _____   **DAY 7**

_____
_____
_____
_____
_____
_____
_____
_____
_____
_____
_____
_____
_____
_____
_____
_____
_____
_____
_____
_____
_____
_____
_____
_____

GOD'S PROMISES

_____
_____
_____
_____

My Weekly Meal Planner & Exercise Log

	BREAKFAST	LUNCH	DINNER

DAY 1

Fasting options:
○ Water only   ○ Liquid only   ○ 24hr
○ 1 meal only   ○ Daniel fast   ○ 16/8

💼 Work Hr:

🌙 Sleep Hr:

Wgt.

Water (circle)

	BREAKFAST	LUNCH	DINNER

DAY 2

Fasting options:
○ Water only   ○ Liquid only   ○ 24hr
○ 1 meal only   ○ Daniel fast   ○ 16/8

💼 Work Hr:

🌙 Sleep Hr:

Wgt.

Water (circle)

	BREAKFAST	LUNCH	DINNER

DAY 3

Fasting options:
○ Water only   ○ Liquid only   ○ 24hr
○ 1 meal only   ○ Daniel fast   ○ 16/8

💼 Work Hr:

🌙 Sleep Hr:

Wgt.

Water (circle)

	BREAKFAST	LUNCH	DINNER

DAY 4

Fasting options:
○ Water only   ○ Liquid only   ○ 24hr
○ 1 meal only   ○ Daniel fast   ○ 16/8

💼 Work Hr:

🌙 Sleep Hr:

Wgt.

Water (circle)

	BREAKFAST	LUNCH	DINNER

DAY 5

Fasting options:
○ Water only   ○ Liquid only   ○ 24hr
○ 1 meal only   ○ Daniel fast   ○ 16/8

💼 Work Hr:

🌙 Sleep Hr:

Wgt.

Water (circle)

	BREAKFAST	**LUNCH**	**DINNER**

DAY 6

Fasting options:
- ○ Water only
- ○ 1 meal only
- ○ Liquid only
- ○ Daniel fast
- ○ 24hr
- ○ 16/8

💼 Work Hr: ___ Wgt. ___

🌙 Sleep Hr: ___

Water (circle) 🥤🥤🥤🥤🥤 🥤🥤🥤🥤🥤

	BREAKFAST	**LUNCH**	**DINNER**

DAY 7

Fasting options:
- ○ Water only
- ○ 1 meal only
- ○ Liquid only
- ○ Daniel fast
- ○ 24hr
- ○ 16/8

💼 Work Hr: ___ Wgt. ___

🌙 Sleep Hr: ___

Water (circle) 🥤🥤🥤🥤🥤 🥤🥤🥤🥤🥤

MY EXERCISE LOG

Day	Exercise/Activity	Body Part	Weight	Time	Distance	Sets	Rep's

NOTES

_____

_____

_____

_____

_____

_____

_____

WHAT'S ON YOUR MIND TODAY?

CONVERSATION WITH MY LORD JOURNALING

WHAT'S ON YOUR MIND TODAY?

CONVERSATION WITH MY LORD JOURNALING

PRAYER REQUESTS

WHO	ISSUE	NOTES	DATE

PRAYER REQUESTS

WHO	ISSUE	NOTES	DATE

...AND I AM SURE OF THIS, THAT HE WHO BEGAN A GOOD WORK IN YOU WILL BRING IT TO COMPLETION AT THE DAY OF JESUS CHRIST.

PHILIPPIANS 1:6

21 DAY DANIEL FAST
WEEK II

"This is the confidence we have in approaching God:
that if we ask anything according to his will, he hears
us. And if we know that he hears us—whatever we
ask—we know that we have what we asked of him.

1 John 5:14-15

GET SPIRITUALY READY

DATE: _____ TO _____

PRAYER THEME AND BIBLE VERSE

BIBLE VERSES

DAY 8

DAY 9

DAY 10

DAY 11

DAY 12

DAY 13

DAY 14

PRAYER REQUEST   Write your prayer requests in the prayer request section.

MY GOALS FOR ......

BIBLE READING PLAN

BODY:

SOUL-MIND:

SPIRIT:

GET PHYSICALLY READY

MEAL PLAN IDEAS : DATE: _____ TO _____

SHOPPING LIST

DAY 8

DAY 9

DAY 10

DAY 11

TO DO

DAY 12

DAY 13

DAY 14

LET LOVE AND

Faithfulness

NEVER LEAVE YOU;
BIND THEM AROUND
YOUR NECK,
WRITE THEM
ON THE TABLET
OF YOUR

Heart.

THEN YOU WILL
WIN FAVOR
AND A GOOD NAME
IN THE SIGHT OF

God
& Man.

PROVERBS 3:3-4.

DEVOTIONAL

SCRIPTURE / READING

WHAT IS GOD SAYING TO ME?

LORD TEACH ME TO

I AM GRATEFUL

LORD I NEED YOUR HELP

PRAYER FOR ME

PRAYER FOR OTHERS

BIBLE STUDY

BOOK: _____   **CHAPTER:** _____

THEME: _____   **DATE:** _____   DAY 8

_____
_____
_____
_____
_____
_____
_____
_____
_____
_____
_____
_____
_____
_____
_____
_____
_____
_____
_____
_____
_____
_____

GOD'S PROMISES

_____
_____
_____
_____

THERE IS NO FEAR IN

Love,

BUT PERFECT LOVE
CASTS OUT FEAR.
FOR FEAR HAS TO DO
—— WITH ——
PUNISHMENT,
AND WHOEVER FEARS
HAS NOT BEEN
PERFECTED
IN LOVE.

1 JOHN 4:18

DEVOTIONAL

SCRIPTURE / READING

WHAT IS GOD SAYING TO ME?

LORD TEACH ME TO

I AM GRATEFUL

LORD I NEED YOUR HELP

PRAYER FOR ME

PRAYER FOR OTHERS

BOOK: _____

CHAPTER: _____

THEME: _____

DATE: _____

DAY 9

_____
_____
_____
_____
_____
_____
_____
_____
_____
_____
_____
_____
_____
_____
_____
_____
_____
_____
_____
_____
_____
_____

GOD'S PROMISES

_____
_____
_____
_____

"NO TEMPTATION HAS OVERTAKEN YOU EXCEPT WHAT IS COMMON TO MANKIND AND GOD IS *Faithful;* HE WILL NOT LET YOU BE TEMPTED BEYOND WHAT YOU CAN BEAR. BUT WHEN YOU ARE TEMPTED, HE WILL ALSO PROVIDE A WAY OUT SO THAT YOU CAN *Endure it."*

1 CORINTHIANS 10:13

DEVOTIONAL

SCRIPTURE / READING

WHAT IS GOD SAYING TO ME?

LORD TEACH ME TO

I AM GRATEFUL

LORD I NEED YOUR HELP

PRAYER FOR ME

PRAYER FOR OTHERS

BIBLE STUDY

BOOK: _____   **CHAPTER:** _____

THEME: _____   **DATE:** _____   **DAY 10**

_____
_____
_____
_____
_____
_____
_____
_____
_____
_____
_____
_____
_____
_____
_____
_____
_____
_____
_____
_____
_____
_____
_____

GOD'S PROMISES
_____
_____
_____
_____

"TRUST IN THE

Lord

WITH ALL YOUR

Heart

AND LEAN NOT ON YOUR OWN

Understanding;

IN ALL YOUR WAYS SUBMIT TO HIM, AND

He will

MAKE YOUR PATHS STRAIGHT."

PROVERBS 3:5-6

DEVOTIONAL

SCRIPTURE / READING

WHAT IS GOD SAYING TO ME?

LORD TEACH ME TO

I AM GRATEFUL

LORD I NEED YOUR HELP

PRAYER FOR ME

PRAYER FOR OTHERS

BOOK: _____   **CHAPTER:** _____

THEME: _____   **DATE:** _____   **DAY 11**

_____
_____
_____
_____
_____
_____
_____
_____
_____
_____
_____
_____
_____
_____
_____
_____
_____
_____
_____
_____
_____
_____
_____

GOD'S PROMISES

_____
_____
_____
_____
_____

"AND THE PRAYER OF *Faith* SHALL SAVE THE SICK AND THE LORD SHALL RAISE HIM UP; AND IF HE HAS COMMITTED SINS, THEY SHALL BE *Forgiven him.*"

JAMES 5:15

DEVOTIONAL

SCRIPTURE / READING

WHAT IS GOD SAYING TO ME?

LORD TEACH ME TO

I AM GRATEFUL

LORD I NEED YOUR HELP

PRAYER FOR ME   PRAYER FOR OTHERS

BIBLE STUDY

BOOK: _____   **CHAPTER:** _____

THEME: _____   **DATE:** _____   **DAY 12**

_____
_____
_____
_____
_____
_____
_____
_____
_____
_____
_____
_____
_____
_____
_____
_____
_____
_____
_____
_____
_____
_____
_____

GOD'S PROMISES

_____
_____
_____
_____

"AND GOD IS ABLE TO *Bless You* ABUNDANTLY, SO THAT IN ALL THINGS AT ALL TIMES, HAVING ALL THAT YOU NEED, YOU WILL ABOUND IN *Every* GOOD WORK."

2 CORINTHIANS 9:8

SCRIPTURE / READING

WHAT IS GOD SAYING TO ME?

LORD TEACH ME TO

I AM GRATEFUL

LORD I NEED YOUR HELP

PRAYER FOR ME

PRAYER FOR OTHERS

BOOK: _____

CHAPTER: _____

THEME: _____

DATE: _____

_____
_____
_____
_____
_____
_____
_____
_____
_____
_____
_____
_____
_____
_____
_____
_____
_____
_____
_____
_____
_____
_____

GOD'S PROMISES

_____
_____
_____
_____
_____

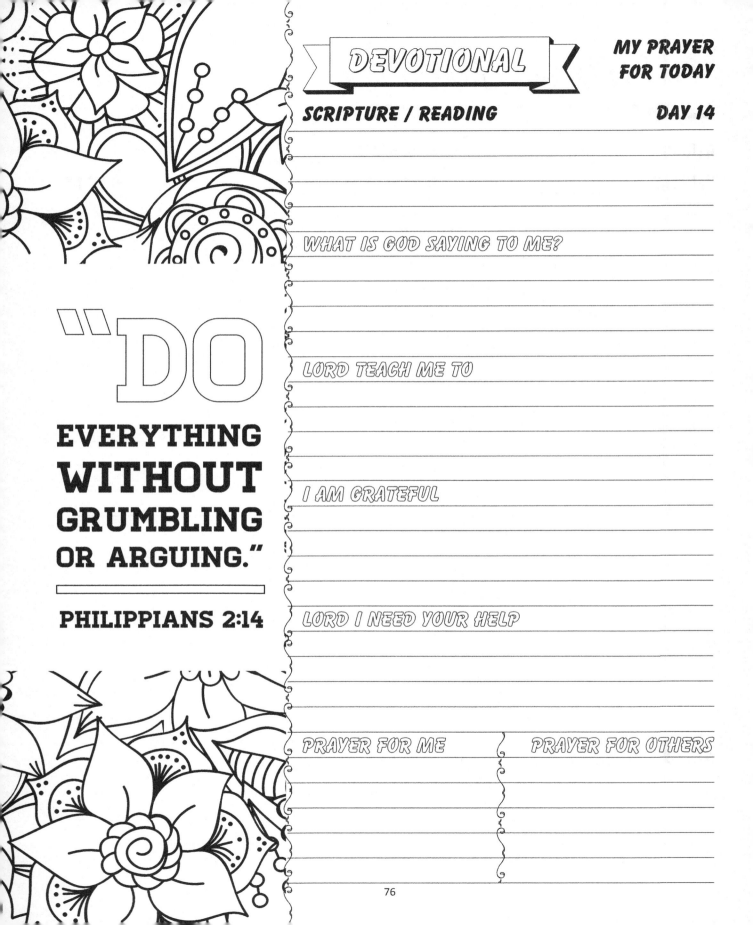

DEVOTIONAL

SCRIPTURE / READING

WHAT IS GOD SAYING TO ME?

LORD TEACH ME TO

I AM GRATEFUL

LORD I NEED YOUR HELP

PRAYER FOR ME   PRAYER FOR OTHERS

"DO EVERYTHING WITHOUT GRUMBLING OR ARGUING."

PHILIPPIANS 2:14

BOOK: _____ **CHAPTER:** _____

THEME: _____ **DATE:** _____ **DAY 14**

_____
_____
_____
_____
_____
_____
_____
_____
_____
_____
_____
_____
_____
_____
_____
_____
_____
_____
_____
_____
_____
_____
_____
_____

GOD'S PROMISES

_____
_____
_____
_____
_____

My Weekly Meal Planner & Exercise Log

	BREAKFAST	LUNCH	DINNER

DAY 8

Fasting options:
○ Water only   ○ Liquid only   ○ 24hr
○ 1 meal only   ○ Daniel fast   ○ 16/8

Work Hr: Sleep Hr: Water (circle)

Wgt.

	BREAKFAST	LUNCH	DINNER

DAY 9

Fasting options:
○ Water only   ○ Liquid only   ○ 24hr
○ 1 meal only   ○ Daniel fast   ○ 16/8

Work Hr: Sleep Hr: Water (circle)

Wgt.

	BREAKFAST	LUNCH	DINNER

DAY 10

Fasting options:
○ Water only   ○ Liquid only   ○ 24hr
○ 1 meal only   ○ Daniel fast   ○ 16/8

Work Hr: Sleep Hr: Water (circle)

Wgt.

	BREAKFAST	LUNCH	DINNER

DAY 11

Fasting options:
○ Water only   ○ Liquid only   ○ 24hr
○ 1 meal only   ○ Daniel fast   ○ 16/8

Work Hr: Sleep Hr: Water (circle)

Wgt.

	BREAKFAST	LUNCH	DINNER

DAY 12

Fasting options:
○ Water only   ○ Liquid only   ○ 24hr
○ 1 meal only   ○ Daniel fast   ○ 16/8

Work Hr: Sleep Hr: Water (circle)

Wgt.

	BREAKFAST	**LUNCH**	**DINNER**

DAY 13

Fasting options:
○ Water only   ○ Liquid only   ○ 24hr
○ 1 meal only   ○ Daniel fast   ○ 16/8

Work Hr: _____   Sleep Hr: _____   Water (circle)

Wgt. _____

	BREAKFAST	**LUNCH**	**DINNER**

DAY 14

Fasting options:
○ Water only   ○ Liquid only   ○ 24hr
○ 1 meal only   ○ Daniel fast   ○ 16/8

Work Hr: _____   Sleep Hr: _____   Water (circle)

Wgt. _____

MY EXERCISE LOG

Day	Exercise/Activity	Body Part	Weight	Time	Distance	Sets	Rep's

NOTES

WHAT'S ON YOUR MIND TODAY?
CONVERSATION WITH MY LORD JOURNALING

WHAT'S ON YOUR MIND TODAY?

CONVERSATION WITH MY LORD JOURNALING

PRAYER REQUESTS

WHO	ISSUE	NOTES	DATE

PRAYER REQUESTS

WHO	ISSUE	NOTES	DATE

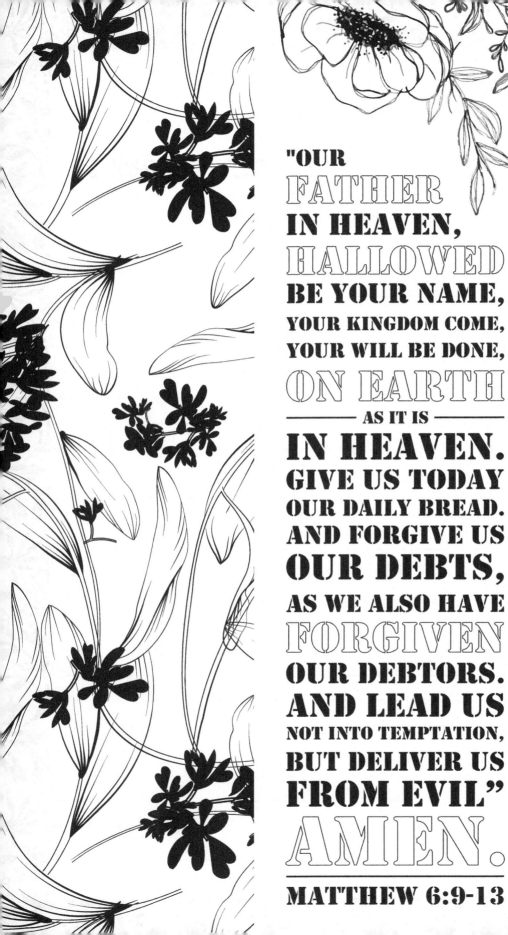

"OUR
FATHER
IN HEAVEN,
HALLOWED
BE YOUR NAME,
YOUR KINGDOM COME,
YOUR WILL BE DONE,
ON EARTH
— AS IT IS —
IN HEAVEN.
GIVE US TODAY
OUR DAILY BREAD.
AND FORGIVE US
OUR DEBTS,
AS WE ALSO HAVE
FORGIVEN
OUR DEBTORS.
AND LEAD US
NOT INTO TEMPTATION,
BUT DELIVER US
FROM EVIL"
AMEN.

MATTHEW 6:9-13

21 DAY DANIEL FAST
WEEK III

"Wait for the Lord; be strong and take heart
and wait for the Lord."

Psalm 27

GET SPIRITUALY READY

PRAYER THEME AND BIBLE VERSE

BIBLE VERSES

DAY 15

DAY 16

DAY 17

DAY 18

DAY 19

DAY 20

DAY 21

PRAYER REQUEST
Write your prayer requests in the prayer request section.

MY GOALS FOR ......

BIBLE READING PLAN

BODY:

SOUL-MIND:

SPIRIT:

GET PHYSICALLY READY

MEAL PLAN IDEAS   DATE: _____ TO _____

SHOPPING LIST

DAY 15

DAY 16

DAY 17

DAY 18

TO DO

DAY 19

DAY 20

DAY 21

"Love THE LORD Your God WITH ALL YOUR Heart AND WITH ALL YOUR soul AND WITH ALL YOUR MIND. THIS IS THE FIRST AND GREATEST COMMANDMENT."

Matthew 22:36-40

DEVOTIONAL

SCRIPTURE / READING

WHAT IS GOD SAYING TO ME?

LORD TEACH ME TO

I AM GRATEFUL

LORD I NEED YOUR HELP

PRAYER FOR ME

PRAYER FOR OTHERS

BIBLE STUDY

BOOK: _____   **CHAPTER:** _____

THEME: _____   **DATE:** _____   **DAY 15**

_____
_____
_____
_____
_____
_____
_____
_____
_____
_____
_____
_____
_____
_____
_____
_____
_____
_____
_____
_____
_____
_____
_____
_____

GOD'S PROMISES

_____
_____
_____
_____

"DO NOT CONFORM TO THE PATTERN OF *This world,* BUT BE TRANSFORMED BY THE RENEWING OF *your mind.* THEN YOU WILL BE ABLE TO TEST AND APPROVE WHAT GOD'S WILL IS— *His good,* PLEASING AND PERFECT WILL."

ROMANS 12:2

WHAT IS GOD SAYING TO ME?

LORD TEACH ME TO

I AM GRATEFUL

LORD I NEED YOUR HELP

PRAYER FOR ME

PRAYER FOR OTHERS

BIBLE STUDY

BOOK: _____   **CHAPTER:** _____

THEME: _____   **DATE:** _____   **DAY 16**

_____
_____
_____
_____
_____
_____
_____
_____
_____
_____
_____
_____
_____
_____
_____
_____
_____
_____
_____
_____
_____
_____
_____
_____
_____

GOD'S PROMISES
_____
_____
_____
_____

"AND THIS *Hope*

WILL NOT LEAD TO DISAPPOINTMENT. FOR WE KNOW HOW DEARLY GOD *loves us,* BECAUSE HE HAS GIVEN US THE *Holy Spirit* TO FILL OUR *hearts* WITH HIS *Love.*"

ROMANS 5:5

WHAT IS GOD SAYING TO ME?

LORD TEACH ME TO

I AM GRATEFUL

LORD I NEED YOUR HELP

PRAYER FOR ME

PRAYER FOR OTHERS

BOOK: _____　　**CHAPTER:** _____

THEME: _____　　**DATE:** _____　　　**DAY 17**

_____
_____
_____
_____
_____
_____
_____
_____
_____
_____
_____
_____
_____
_____
_____
_____
_____
_____
_____
_____
_____
_____
_____
_____
_____

GOD'S PROMISES

_____
_____
_____
_____

"BUT STORE UP FOR YOURSELVES TREASURES IN *Heaven,* **WHERE NEITHER MOTH NOR RUST DESTROYS, AND WHERE THIEVES DO NOT BREAK IN OR STEAL."**

Mattew 6:20

SCRIPTURE / READING

DAY 18

WHAT IS GOD SAYING TO ME?

LORD TEACH ME TO

I AM GRATEFUL

LORD I NEED YOUR HELP

PRAYER FOR ME

PRAYER FOR OTHERS

BIBLE STUDY

BOOK: _____   **CHAPTER:** _____

THEME: _____   **DATE:** _____   **DAY 18**

_____
_____
_____
_____
_____
_____
_____
_____
_____
_____
_____
_____
_____
_____
_____
_____
_____
_____
_____
_____
_____
_____
_____
_____
_____

GOD'S PROMISES

_____
_____
_____
_____
_____

"FEAR NOT: FOR I HAVE REDEEMED YOU, I HAVE CALLED YOU BY YOUR NAME; YOU ARE MINE."

ISAIAH 43:1

SCRIPTURE / READING

WHAT IS GOD SAYING TO ME?

LORD TEACH ME TO

I AM GRATEFUL

LORD I NEED YOUR HELP

PRAYER FOR ME

PRAYER FOR OTHERS

BOOK: _____   **CHAPTER:** _____

THEME: _____   **DATE:** _____   DAY 19

_____
_____
_____
_____
_____
_____
_____
_____
_____
_____
_____
_____
_____
_____
_____
_____
_____
_____
_____
_____
_____
_____
_____
_____

GOD'S PROMISES

_____
_____
_____
_____
_____

"AND WITHOUT

IT IS IMPOSSIBLE TO
PLEASE GOD,
**BECAUSE ANYONE
WHO COMES TO HIM
MUST BELIEVE THAT
HE EXISTS AND THAT
HE REWARDS THOSE
WHO EARNESTLY**

seek him"

HEBREWS 11:6

DEVOTIONAL

SCRIPTURE / READING

WHAT IS GOD SAYING TO ME?

LORD TEACH ME TO

I AM GRATEFUL

LORD I NEED YOUR HELP

PRAYER FOR ME

PRAYER FOR OTHERS

BOOK: _____   **CHAPTER:** _____

THEME: _____   **DATE:** _____   **DAY 20**

_____

_____

_____

_____

_____

_____

_____

_____

_____

_____

_____

_____

_____

_____

_____

_____

_____

_____

_____

_____

_____

_____

GOD'S PROMISES

_____

_____

_____

_____

"BUT AS FOR YOU, BE STRONG AND DO NOT GIVE UP, FOR YOUR WORK WILL BE REWARDED."

2 CHRONICLES 15:7

SCRIPTURE / READING

WHAT IS GOD SAYING TO ME?

LORD TEACH ME TO

I AM GRATEFUL

LORD I NEED YOUR HELP

PRAYER FOR ME

PRAYER FOR OTHERS

BOOK: _____   **CHAPTER:** _____

THEME: _____   **DATE:** _____   **DAY 21**

_____
_____
_____
_____
_____
_____
_____
_____
_____
_____
_____
_____
_____
_____
_____
_____
_____
_____
_____
_____
_____
_____
_____

GOD'S PROMISES

_____
_____
_____
_____

MY WEEKLY MEAL PLANNER & EXERCISE LOG

	BREAKFAST	LUNCH	DINNER

DAY 15

Fasting options:
- ○ Water only
- ○ 1 meal only
- ○ Liquid only
- ○ Daniel fast
- ○ 24hr
- ○ 16/8

Work Hr: Sleep Hr: Water (circle)

Wgt.

	BREAKFAST	LUNCH	DINNER

DAY 16

Fasting options:
- ○ Water only
- ○ 1 meal only
- ○ Liquid only
- ○ Daniel fast
- ○ 24hr
- ○ 16/8

Work Hr: Sleep Hr: Water (circle)

Wgt.

	BREAKFAST	LUNCH	DINNER

DAY 17

Fasting options:
- ○ Water only
- ○ 1 meal only
- ○ Liquid only
- ○ Daniel fast
- ○ 24hr
- ○ 16/8

Work Hr: Sleep Hr: Water (circle)

Wgt.

	BREAKFAST	LUNCH	DINNER

DAY 18

Fasting options:
- ○ Water only
- ○ 1 meal only
- ○ Liquid only
- ○ Daniel fast
- ○ 24hr
- ○ 16/8

Work Hr: Sleep Hr: Water (circle)

Wgt.

	BREAKFAST	LUNCH	DINNER

DAY 19

Fasting options:
- ○ Water only
- ○ 1 meal only
- ○ Liquid only
- ○ Daniel fast
- ○ 24hr
- ○ 16/8

Work Hr: Sleep Hr: Water (circle)

Wgt.

	BREAKFAST	LUNCH	DINNER

DAY 20

Fasting options:
○ Water only   ○ Liquid only   ○ 24hr
○ 1 meal only   ○ Daniel fast   ○ 16/8

Work Hr: _____   Sleep Hr: _____   Water (circle)

Wgt. _____

	BREAKFAST	LUNCH	DINNER

DAY 21

Fasting options:
○ Water only   ○ Liquid only   ○ 24hr
○ 1 meal only   ○ Daniel fast   ○ 16/8

Work Hr: _____   Sleep Hr: _____   Water (circle)

Wgt. _____

MY EXERCISE LOG

Day	Exercise/Activity	Body Part	Weight	Time	Distance	Sets	Rep's

NOTES

WHAT'S ON YOUR MIND TODAY?
CONVERSATION WITH MY LORD JOURNALING

WHAT'S ON YOUR MIND TODAY?

CONVERSATION WITH MY LORD JOURNALING

PRAYER REQUESTS

WHO	ISSUE	NOTES	DATE

PRAYER REQUESTS

WHO	ISSUE	NOTES	DATE

DAY 22: A NEW YOU: LET YOUR LIFE BE CHANGED

Verse for the day:

"I have been crucified with Christ and I no longer live, but Christ lives in me. The life I live in the body I live by faith in the Son of God who loved me and gave himself for me."
~Galatians 2:20 (NIV)

WHAT ABOUT YOU

You have completed the twenty-one days of fasting. It is impossible for you to not have experienced changes in your life during this time. In thinking about these changes, what benefits have you derived from them? How have you changed from the inside out?

MAKING IT PERSONAL

Now that the 'official' period of fasting is over, come together with those who fasted with you and with those who encouraged you along the way (even if they didn't participate in the fast). Talk about the changes that took place in your life and commit to continuing the journey together so that you can all continue to grow in your faith, treat your bodies as temples of the Holy Spirit, and grow in your knowledge of the Word of God. After you have completed the 21 Daniel Fast, you have an option to continue once a week or as you wish. The next section is there for you as an option to record your prayer and fasting after the official Daniel Fast.

PRAYER AND PRAISE

PRAY: Father in heaven, Thank You so much for these last three weeks. Thank You for letting me see myself through Your eyes. Thank You for letting me learn more about who I was created to be and how my body is designed to work. Thank You for letting me come to a greater understanding of Your Word and that it is real and lasting; that it is relevant and useful now and always. Give me the strength and heart to continue on this journey so that I will never stop learning and never stop longing to know You better.

IN JESUS' NAME I PRAY, AMEN.

SHARE YOUR TESTIMONY

WRITE DOWN HOW THE 21 DAY DANIEL FAST HAS CHANGED YOUR LIFE

_____

_____

_____

_____

_____

_____

_____

_____

_____

_____

_____

_____

_____

_____

_____

_____

_____

_____

_____

_____

_____

_____

_____

_____

_____

"Oh, Lord GOD!

You have made the heavens and earth by Your great power and OUTSTRETCHED ARM.

Nothing is too difficult for YOU!

-Jeremiah 32:17

HUNGRY FOR GOD

MY PRAYER & FASTING DAY

Do not be anxious about anything, but in every situation, by prayer
and petition, with thanksgiving, present your requests to God. And
the peace of God, which transcends all understanding, will guard
your hearts and your minds in Christ Jesus.

Philippians 4:6-7

DEVOTIONAL

MY PRAYER FOR TODAY

SCRIPTURE / READING   **DATE:** _____

_____

_____

_____

WHAT IS GOD SAYING TO ME? _____

_____

_____

_____

LORD TEACH ME TO _____   **I AM GRATEFUL** _____

_____

_____

LORD I NEED YOUR HELP _____

_____

_____

_____

_____

PRAYER FOR ME _____   **PRAYER FOR OTHERS** _____

_____

_____

_____

FASTING OPTIONS: ○ WATER ONLY   ○ LIQUID ONLY   ○ ONE MEAL ONLY   ○ DANIEL FAST   ○ 24HR

NOTES: _____

_____

_____

DEVOTIONAL

MY PRAYER FOR TODAY

SCRIPTURE / READING

DATE: _____

_____
_____
_____
_____

WHAT IS GOD SAYING TO ME? _____
_____
_____
_____

LORD TEACH ME TO _____   **I AM GRATEFUL** _____
_____   _____
_____   _____
_____   _____

LORD I NEED YOUR HELP _____
_____
_____
_____
_____

PRAYER FOR ME _____   **PRAYER FOR OTHERS** _____
_____   _____
_____   _____
_____   _____

FASTING OPTIONS: ◯ WATER ONLY   ◯ LIQUID ONLY   ◯ ONE MEAL ONLY   ◯ DANIEL FAST   ◯ 24HR

NOTES:
_____
_____
_____

DEVOTIONAL

MY PRAYER FOR TODAY

SCRIPTURE / READING

DATE: _____

_____
_____
_____
_____

(WHAT IS GOD SAYING TO ME?) _____

_____
_____
_____
_____

(LORD TEACH ME TO) _____   (I AM GRATEFUL) _____

_____   _____
_____   _____
_____   _____

(LORD I NEED YOUR HELP) _____

_____
_____
_____
_____
_____

(PRAYER FOR ME) _____   (PRAYER FOR OTHERS) _____

_____   _____
_____   _____
_____   _____

FASTING OPTIONS: ○ WATER ONLY   ○ LIQUID ONLY   ○ ONE MEAL ONLY   ○ DANIEL FAST   ○ 24HR

NOTES:
_____
_____
_____

DEVOTIONAL

MY PRAYER FOR TODAY

SCRIPTURE / READING

DATE: _____

_____
_____
_____
_____

(WHAT IS GOD SAYING TO ME?) _____
_____
_____
_____

(LORD TEACH ME TO) _____   (I AM GRATEFUL) _____
_____
_____
_____

(LORD I NEED YOUR HELP) _____
_____
_____
_____
_____

(PRAYER FOR ME) _____   (PRAYER FOR OTHERS) _____
_____
_____
_____

FASTING OPTIONS: ○ WATER ONLY ○ LIQUID ONLY ○ ONE MEAL ONLY ○ DANIEL FAST ○ 24HR

NOTES: _____
_____
_____
_____

DEVOTIONAL

SCRIPTURE / READING

DATE: _____

_____

_____

_____

_____

WHAT IS GOD SAYING TO ME?

_____

_____

_____

_____

LORD TEACH ME TO _____   ### I AM GRATEFUL _____

_____

_____

LORD I NEED YOUR HELP _____

_____

_____

_____

_____

PRAYER FOR ME _____   ### PRAYER FOR OTHERS _____

_____

_____

_____

FASTING OPTIONS: ○ WATER ONLY   ○ LIQUID ONLY   ○ ONE MEAL ONLY   ○ DANIEL FAST   ○ 24HR

NOTES:

_____

_____

_____

DEVOTIONAL

SCRIPTURE / READING

DATE: _____

_____

_____

_____

_____

WHAT IS GOD SAYING TO ME?

_____

_____

_____

LORD TEACH ME TO _____   **I AM GRATEFUL** _____

_____

_____

_____

LORD I NEED YOUR HELP _____

_____

_____

_____

_____

PRAYER FOR ME _____   **PRAYER FOR OTHERS** _____

_____

_____

_____

FASTING OPTIONS: ◯ WATER ONLY   ◯ LIQUID ONLY   ◯ ONE MEAL ONLY   ◯ DANIEL FAST   ◯ 24HR

NOTES:

_____

_____

DEVOTIONAL

MY PRAYER FOR TODAY

SCRIPTURE / READING   **DATE:** _____

_____

_____

_____

_____

WHAT IS GOD SAYING TO ME? _____

_____

_____

_____

LORD TEACH ME TO _____   **I AM GRATEFUL** _____

_____   _____

_____   _____

_____   _____

LORD I NEED YOUR HELP _____

_____

_____

_____

_____

PRAYER FOR ME _____   **PRAYER FOR OTHERS** _____

_____   _____

_____   _____

_____   _____

FASTING OPTIONS: ◯ WATER ONLY   ◯ LIQUID ONLY   ◯ ONE MEAL ONLY   ◯ DANIEL FAST   ◯ 24HR

NOTES:

_____

_____

_____

DEVOTIONAL

MY PRAYER FOR TODAY

SCRIPTURE / READING

DATE: _____

_____
_____
_____
_____

WHAT IS GOD SAYING TO ME?
_____
_____
_____
_____

LORD TEACH ME TO _____

I AM GRATEFUL _____

LORD I NEED YOUR HELP
_____
_____
_____
_____
_____

PRAYER FOR ME _____

PRAYER FOR OTHERS _____

FASTING OPTIONS: ◯ WATER ONLY ◯ LIQUID ONLY ◯ ONE MEAL ONLY ◯ DANIEL FAST ◯ 24HR

NOTES:
_____
_____

DEVOTIONAL

MY PRAYER FOR TODAY

SCRIPTURE / READING

DATE: _____

_____
_____
_____
_____

WHAT IS GOD SAYING TO ME? _____
_____
_____
_____

LORD TEACH ME TO _____ **I AM GRATEFUL** _____
_____
_____
_____

LORD I NEED YOUR HELP _____
_____
_____
_____
_____

PRAYER FOR ME _____ **PRAYER FOR OTHERS** _____
_____
_____
_____

FASTING OPTIONS: ○ WATER ONLY ○ LIQUID ONLY ○ ONE MEAL ONLY ○ DANIEL FAST ○ 24HR

NOTES:
_____
_____
_____

DEVOTIONAL

MY PRAYER FOR TODAY

SCRIPTURE / READING

DATE: _____

_____
_____
_____

WHAT IS GOD SAYING TO ME? _____
_____
_____
_____

LORD TEACH ME TO _____   **I AM GRATEFUL** _____
_____
_____
_____

LORD I NEED YOUR HELP _____
_____
_____
_____

PRAYER FOR ME _____   **PRAYER FOR OTHERS** _____
_____
_____
_____

FASTING OPTIONS: ○ WATER ONLY   ○ LIQUID ONLY   ○ ONE MEAL ONLY   ○ DANIEL FAST   ○ 24HR

NOTES:
_____
_____
_____

DEVOTIONAL

MY PRAYER FOR TODAY

SCRIPTURE / READING

DATE: _____

_____

_____

_____

_____

WHAT IS GOD SAYING TO ME?

_____

_____

_____

_____

LORD TEACH ME TO _____

I AM GRATEFUL _____

_____

_____

LORD I NEED YOUR HELP

_____

_____

_____

_____

PRAYER FOR ME _____

PRAYER FOR OTHERS _____

_____

_____

_____

FASTING OPTIONS: ○ WATER ONLY   ○ LIQUID ONLY   ○ ONE MEAL ONLY   ○ DANIEL FAST   ○ 24HR

NOTES:

_____

_____

_____

DEVOTIONAL

MY PRAYER FOR TODAY

SCRIPTURE / READING

DATE: _____

_____
_____
_____
_____

WHAT IS GOD SAYING TO ME? _____
_____
_____
_____

LORD TEACH ME TO _____   **I AM GRATEFUL** _____
_____
_____
_____

LORD I NEED YOUR HELP _____
_____
_____
_____
_____

PRAYER FOR ME _____   **PRAYER FOR OTHERS** _____
_____
_____
_____

FASTING OPTIONS: ○ WATER ONLY   ○ LIQUID ONLY   ○ ONE MEAL ONLY   ○ DANIEL FAST   ○ 24HR

NOTES:
_____
_____
_____

DEVOTIONAL

SCRIPTURE / READING

DATE: _____

_____
_____
_____
_____

WHAT IS GOD SAYING TO ME? _____
_____
_____
_____

LORD TEACH ME TO _____   **I AM GRATEFUL** _____
_____
_____
_____

LORD I NEED YOUR HELP _____
_____
_____
_____
_____

PRAYER FOR ME _____   **PRAYER FOR OTHERS** _____
_____
_____
_____
_____

FASTING OPTIONS: ○ WATER ONLY   ○ LIQUID ONLY   ○ ONE MEAL ONLY   ○ DANIEL FAST   ○ 24HR

NOTES:
_____
_____
_____

DEVOTIONAL

SCRIPTURE / READING

DATE: _____

_____

_____

_____

_____

WHAT IS GOD SAYING TO ME? _____

_____

_____

_____

LORD TEACH ME TO _____   **I AM GRATEFUL** _____

_____   _____

_____   _____

LORD I NEED YOUR HELP _____

_____

_____

_____

_____

PRAYER FOR ME _____   **PRAYER FOR OTHERS** _____

_____   _____

_____   _____

_____   _____

FASTING OPTIONS: ◯ WATER ONLY   ◯ LIQUID ONLY   ◯ ONE MEAL ONLY   ◯ DANIEL FAST   ◯ 24HR

NOTES: _____

_____

_____

_____

DEVOTIONAL

MY PRAYER FOR TODAY

SCRIPTURE / READING

DATE: _____

_____
_____
_____
_____

WHAT IS GOD SAYING TO ME? _____

_____
_____
_____

LORD TEACH ME TO _____   **I AM GRATEFUL** _____

_____
_____
_____

LORD I NEED YOUR HELP _____

_____
_____
_____
_____

PRAYER FOR ME _____   **PRAYER FOR OTHERS** _____

_____
_____
_____

FASTING OPTIONS: ○ WATER ONLY ○ LIQUID ONLY ○ ONE MEAL ONLY ○ DANIEL FAST ○ 24HR

NOTES:
_____
_____
_____

DEVOTIONAL

MY PRAYER FOR TODAY

SCRIPTURE / READING

DATE: _____

_____

_____

_____

(WHAT IS GOD SAYING TO ME?) _____

_____

_____

_____

(LORD TEACH ME TO) _____   (I AM GRATEFUL) _____

_____

_____

(LORD I NEED YOUR HELP) _____

_____

_____

_____

_____

(PRAYER FOR ME) _____   (PRAYER FOR OTHERS) _____

_____

_____

_____

FASTING OPTIONS: ◯ WATER ONLY   ◯ LIQUID ONLY   ◯ ONE MEAL ONLY   ◯ DANIEL FAST   ◯ 24HR

NOTES:

_____

_____

DEVOTIONAL

MY PRAYER FOR TODAY

SCRIPTURE / READING

DATE: _____

_____
_____
_____
_____

WHAT IS GOD SAYING TO ME? _____
_____
_____
_____
_____

LORD TEACH ME TO _____   **I AM GRATEFUL** _____
_____
_____
_____

LORD I NEED YOUR HELP _____
_____
_____
_____
_____

PRAYER FOR ME _____   **PRAYER FOR OTHERS** _____
_____
_____
_____
_____

FASTING OPTIONS: ◯ WATER ONLY   ◯ LIQUID ONLY   ◯ ONE MEAL ONLY   ◯ DANIEL FAST   ◯ 24HR

NOTES:
_____
_____
_____

DEVOTIONAL

MY PRAYER FOR TODAY

SCRIPTURE / READING

DATE: _____

_____
_____
_____
_____

(**WHAT IS GOD SAYING TO ME?**) _____
_____
_____
_____

(**LORD TEACH ME TO**) _____   (**I AM GRATEFUL**) _____
_____
_____
_____

(**LORD I NEED YOUR HELP**) _____
_____
_____
_____

(**PRAYER FOR ME**) _____   (**PRAYER FOR OTHERS**) _____
_____
_____
_____

FASTING OPTIONS: ◯ WATER ONLY   ◯ LIQUID ONLY   ◯ ONE MEAL ONLY   ◯ DANIEL FAST   ◯ 24HR

NOTES:
_____
_____
_____

DEVOTIONAL

MY PRAYER FOR TODAY

SCRIPTURE / READING   **DATE:** _____

_____

_____

_____

_____

WHAT IS GOD SAYING TO ME? _____

_____

_____

LORD TEACH ME TO _____   **I AM GRATEFUL** _____

_____   _____

_____   _____

_____   _____

LORD I NEED YOUR HELP _____

_____

_____

_____

_____

PRAYER FOR ME _____   **PRAYER FOR OTHERS** _____

_____   _____

_____   _____

_____   _____

FASTING OPTIONS: ◯ WATER ONLY   ◯ LIQUID ONLY   ◯ ONE MEAL ONLY   ◯ DANIEL FAST   ◯ 24HR

NOTES:

_____

_____

DEVOTIONAL

SCRIPTURE / READING

DATE: _____

_____
_____
_____
_____

WHAT IS GOD SAYING TO ME? _____
_____
_____
_____
_____

LORD TEACH ME TO _____   **I AM GRATEFUL** _____
_____   _____
_____   _____
_____   _____

LORD I NEED YOUR HELP _____
_____
_____
_____
_____

PRAYER FOR ME _____   **PRAYER FOR OTHERS** _____
_____   _____
_____   _____
_____   _____

FASTING OPTIONS: ○ WATER ONLY   ○ LIQUID ONLY   ○ ONE MEAL ONLY   ○ DANIEL FAST   ○ 24HR

NOTES:
_____
_____
_____

DEVOTIONAL

MY PRAYER FOR TODAY

SCRIPTURE / READING

DATE: _____

_____

_____

_____

_____

(WHAT IS GOD SAYING TO ME?) _____

_____

_____

_____

(LORD TEACH ME TO) _____ (I AM GRATEFUL) _____

_____

_____

_____

(LORD I NEED YOUR HELP) _____

_____

_____

_____

_____

(PRAYER FOR ME) _____ (PRAYER FOR OTHERS) _____

_____

_____

_____

_____

FASTING OPTIONS: ○ WATER ONLY ○ LIQUID ONLY ○ ONE MEAL ONLY ○ DANIEL FAST ○ 24HR

NOTES:

_____

_____

_____

DEVOTIONAL

MY PRAYER FOR TODAY

SCRIPTURE / READING

DATE: _____

_____
_____
_____
_____

WHAT IS GOD SAYING TO ME? _____

_____
_____
_____

LORD TEACH ME TO _____   **I AM GRATEFUL** _____

_____
_____
_____

LORD I NEED YOUR HELP _____

_____
_____
_____
_____

PRAYER FOR ME _____   **PRAYER FOR OTHERS** _____

_____
_____
_____

FASTING OPTIONS: ◯ WATER ONLY   ◯ LIQUID ONLY   ◯ ONE MEAL ONLY   ◯ DANIEL FAST   ◯ 24HR

NOTES:

_____
_____

ALWAYS BE JOYFUL. NEVER STOP PRAYING. BE THANKFUL IN ALL CIRCUMSTANCES, FOR THIS IS GOD'S WILL FOR YOU WHO BELONG TO CHRIST JESUS.

1 THESSALONIANS 5:16-18

21 DAY DANIEL FAST
PRAYER & TOOLBOX

"Devote yourselves to prayer,
being watchful and thankful."

Colossians 4:2

Suggested Meal Options

and

Daniel Fast Food List

come from the

Paradise Garden Vegan Cookbook

by MARIA

and are available at

www.HealthyLivingMinistry.org

www.Danielfast.org

What to Eat During Daniel Fast
21 Days Daniel Fast Food List

FOODS TO EAT
yes!

ALL FRUITS
(fresh, frozen, dried, juiced, or canned)
Apples, Apricots, Avocados, Bananas, Blackberries, Blueberries, Cantaloupe, Cherries, Coconuts, Cranberries, Dates, Figs, Grapefruit, Grapes, Guava, Honeydew melons, Kiwi, Lemons, Limes, Mangoes, Melons, Nectarines, Oranges, Papayas, Peaches, Pears, Pineapples, Plums, Prunes, Raisins, Raspberries, Strawberries, Tangerines, Watermelon.

ALL WHOLE GRAINS
(preferably organic)
Amaranth, Barley, Brown rice, Millet, Quinoa, Oats (groats soaked), Whole Wheat.

ALL LEGUMES
(preferably organic, raw, unsalted and soaked/sprouted)
Black beans, Black eyed peas, Cannellini beans, Garbanzo beans (chickpeas), Great northern beans, Kidney beans, Lentils, Mung beans, Pinto beans, and Split peas.

BEVERAGES
Water, Homemade Vegetable juice, Green Smoothies, Homemade Nuts Milks.

ALL VEGETABLES
(fresh, frozen, dried, juiced, or canned)
Artichokes, Asparagus, Beets, Broccoli, Brussel sprouts, Cabbage, Carrots, Cauliflower, Celery, Collard greens, Corn, Cucumbers, Eggplant, Green beans, Kale, Leeks, Lettuce, Mushrooms, Mustard greens, Okra, Onions, Parsley, Peppers, Potatoes, Radishes, Rutabagas, Scallions, Spinach, Sprouts, Squash, Sweet potatoes, Tomatoes, Turnips, Yams, Zucchini.

ALL QUALITY OILS
Avocado, Coconut, Grapeseed, Olive, Peanut, Sesame, and Walnut.

SPICES AND CONDIMENTS
Herbs, Spices, Salt, Pepper, Seasonings, Bragg's Liquid Aminos.

ALL NUTS & SEEDS
(preferably organic, raw, unsalted and soaked/sprouted)
All nuts (raw, unsalted), Almonds, Cashews, Chia seed, Flaxseed, Macadamia nuts, Peanuts, Pecans, Pine nuts, Walnuts, Pumpkin seeds, Sesame seeds, and Sunflower seeds; Unsweetened almond milk. Nut butters are also included.

FOODS TO AVOID
no!

All Meat & Animal Products
Bacon, Beef, Buffalo, Eggs, Fish, Lamb, Poultry, Pork.

All Dairy Products
Butter, Cheese, Cream, Milk, Yogurt.

All Sweeteners
Agave Nectar, Artificial Sweeteners, Brown Rice Syrup, Cane Juice, Honey, Molasses, Raw Sugar, Syrups, Stevia, Sugar.

All Leavened Bread & Yeast
Baked Goods & Bread.

All Refined & Processed Food Products
Artificial Flavorings, Chemicals, Food Additives, Preservatives, White Flour, White Rice.

All Deep-Fried Foods
Corn Chips, French Fries, Potato Chips. All Solid Fats Lard, Margarine, and Shortening.

Beverages
Alcohol, Carbonated Drinks, Coffee, Energy Drinks, Teas.

Suggested Meal Options

Breakfast

Green Smoothies, fresh homemade juices, fruit bowl, old fashion apple oatmeal, granola, steel-cut oats with mix berries and nuts, apple or banana with natural peanut or almond butter.

Appetizers & Sauces

Hummus, eggplant dip with garlic, herbal sauce, mint sauce, fresh vegetables, salads with vinaigrette, pomegranate vinaigrette, tahini sauce, roasted artichokes, guacamole, olive spreads, Pico de Gallo, Passover herbal sauce, herbal green sauce, "schug", sauerkraut, coconut buckwheat porridge, cauliflower pizza bites, cashew stuffed cucumbers, vegan stuffed mushroom caps, falafel bites, roasted cauliflower, roasted vegetables (*potatoes, carrots, beets, parsnips, cherry tomatoes, onions, peppers, garlic, broccoli, mushrooms, cauliflower, eggplant, okra, green beans, Brussel sprouts*), chickpea salad, southwest corn and black bean salad, green barley salad with arugula, stuffed grape leaves with quinoa.

Soups

Vegan sancocho, Bulgarian white bean soup "bob chorba", minestrone soup, tomato basil soup, orange lentils, green power soup, tomato basil soup, mushroom barley soup, corn and red potato chowder, leek potato soup, Russian borscht soup, carrot and ginger soup, vegan black bean soup, Thai pumpkin soup.

Salads

Vegan eggless salad, carrot salad, mint Asian apple slaw, cranberry cilantro quinoa salad, chopped kale salad, green nut salad with pomegranate, balsamic barley berry salad, eggplant salad, 7 species barley-pomegranates salad, many colors" joseph salad, Thai papaya green salad, chickpea salad, vegetable salad with avocado, tabbouleh, southwest corn & black bean salad, strawberry spinach salad.

Suggested Meal Options

Entrees

Bon Appetit!

STEWS, WRAPS, AND MORE:
Vegan chili, Spanish paella,
habichuelas guisadas,
cauliflower and spinach curry,
lady finger stew, oven roasted falafel,
Egyptian fava beans,
falafel garden bowls,
barley leek mushroom stew,
Persian vegan herb stew, "ghormeh sabzi",
Portobello mushrooms,
lettuce wrap,
quinoa vegetable stuffed bell peppers,
bean curry & rice.

Snacks & Desserts

Baked apple
Spicy mixed nuts
Pina colada sorbet
Peanut butter with apple
Dates with walnuts.

Wraps & Burgers

Vegan tuna salad wrap,
vegan cheeseburger,
vegan sloppy joe,
chickpea shawarma lettuce wrap,
Mediterranean lettuce wrap,
cauliflower chicken-wings,
Portobello mushroom over quinoa,
grilled eggplant with quinoa,
grilled cauliflower with green barley salad,
zucchini pasta,
grilled veggie-tofu skewers over beans & rice,
grilled vegetarian stuffed zucchini,
tofu with coleslaw,
lentil meatloaf with steamed vegetables,
green bean stew, wild rice casserole, tofu
breakfast scramble,
vegetables with brown rice,
Spanish rice with zucchini,
spaghetti with roasted veggie meatball
in olive tomato garlic sauce,
paradise power bowl.

What is a Paradise Garden Power Bowl?

It is a yummy, delicious "all-in-one" layered meal that is packed with a variety of greens veggies, sprouts, beans, rice, plant-based protein and topped off with grains, nuts, seeds and drizzled with your favorite sauce. You can eat mindfully and create your own personalized bowl to enjoy all the savory flavors and textures that nature has to offer. Because of the combination of grains, greens and beans, you are getting a bowl full of complete proteins – all the essential amino acids that your body needs will be provided.

Here are some inspirational ideas and a step-by-step guide to get you started. Keep in mind that it can be eaten anytime but during the fasting time, you may have to omit and ingredients that are not permitted during the fast. For example: white rice, certain condiments, pasta, mayonnaise, etc.

HOW TO BULID YOUR OWN "PARADISE GARDEN POWER BOWL"©

(TAKEN FROM PARADISE GARDEN VEGAN COOKBOOK)

STEP 1

PICK YOUR CUISINE :
Decide what type of cuisine you would like to create!

STEP 2

PICK YOUR BASE :
Cooked or steamed: Rice, corn, grits, beans, barley, couscous, chickpeas, buckwheat, bread, bulgur, quinoa, farro, freekeh, kamut, millet, sorghum or amaranth, oats, noodles, pasta, macaroni, taro, plantain, quinoa, beans, peas & lentils.

STEP 3

PICK YOUR VEGGIES (RAW, STEAMED, ETC.) :
Chopped /Shredded Veggies work best: kale, romaine, bok choy, spinach, zucchini, cabbage, mushrooms, carrots, cucumbers, mixed greens, arugula, red cabbage, sprouts, avocado, peppers, broccoli, green onions, radish, watercress, tomatoes, red onion, garlic, ginger, celery, cauliflower, red pepper, mushrooms, green peas, leeks, sprouted beans, beets, squash, artichoke, edamame.

YOU CAN ALSO ADD A PROBIOTIC OR PICKLED FOOD:
Or diced fruits: pineapple, berry, lemon, orange, mango, coconut, peach, cranberry, apple, bamboo shoots, melons, lychee, cactus fruit, pomegranate, fig, berry, dates, cantaloupe, honeydew, cherry, kiwi.

HOW TO BULID YOUR OWN
"PARADISE GARDEN POWER BOWL"©

(TAKEN FROM PARADISE GARDEN VEGAN COOKBOOK)

STEP 4

ADD YOUR PROTEIN OR MEATLESS OPTION :
Baked Tofu, Portabella or Shiitake Mushrooms, Seitan Steak-chicken-Marinated Tempeh, Veggie Burger, Nut Burger, Jack Fruit, Coconut Meat.

STEP 5

PICK YOUR GOODIES :
Seeds and Nuts: Chia Seeds, Flaxseed, Hemp Seeds, Poppy Seed, Pumpkin Seeds, Sesame Seeds, Safflower, Sunflower, Almond, Walnut, Brazil Nut, Cashew, Chestnuts, Hazelnut, Pine Nut, Macadamia,
Crushed taro chips, Nori strips, Wasabi peas.

STEP 6

PICK YOUR DIP AND/OR SAUCE/DRESSING :
a) **Your sauce:** Marinara, Tomato Sauce, Cashews/Nut, Pizza Sauce, Lemon-Tahini, Worcestershire Sauce, Salsa, Chilli Mango, Garlic Lemon Sauce.

b) **Your dips:** Guacamole, Artichoke Spinach Dip, Eggplant Pepper Spread, White Bean Pâté, Olive Tampende, Baba Ganoush, Hummus Dip, Tahini-Garlic Sauce, Passover Herbal Sauce, Passover Horseradish Sauce, Herbal Green Sauce, Ginger-Lime Hummus, Mango Salsa, Basil Pesto.

c) **Oil-free dressings:** Miso Ginger Creamy Dressing, Russian Dijon Balsamic Dressing, Creamy Avocado Fresh Herb Dressing, Creamy Cashew Herb Dressing, Lemon-Tahini Dressing, Cumin-Lime Tahini Dressing, Vinaigrette.

d) **Oil dressings:** (only sugar and sweetener free are allowed) Greek, Italian, Asian Spicy Mango Dressing, Ponzu Sauce, Tahini Orange Dressing, Honey Garlic Mustard Dressing, Thai Red Curry Lemongrass, Vinegar-Olive Oil, Lemon-Basil Vinaigrette, Ginger-Garlic, Chipotle Vinaigrette, Dijon Balsamic Dressing.

STEP 7

PICK YOUR SEASONINGS :
Salt, Black Pepper, Curry, Garlic, Onion, Turmeric, Garam Masala, Cayenne, Chili Powder, Smoked Jalapeño Peppers, Mustard, Thyme, Red Pepper, Ginger, Mint, Dill, Oregano, Basil, Cilantro, Parsley, Chives, Rosemary, Cumin.

Bible Study Plan Ideas

PLAN 1	PLAN 2	PLAN 3	PLAN 4	PLAN 5	PLAN 6
Daniel 1-2	Rom 1	Phil 1	Luke 1-2	Esther 1-2	1 Cor 1-3
Daniel 3-4	Rom 2	Phil 2	Luke 3-5	Esther 3-4	1 Cor 4-5
Daniel 5-6	Rom 3	Phil 3	Luke 6-8	Esther 4-5	1 Cor 5-7
Daniel 7-8	Rom 4	Phil 4	Luke 9-10	Esther 6-8	1 Cor 8-10
Daniel 9-10	Rom 5	Col 1	Luke 11	Esther 8-10	1 Cor 11-12
Daniel 11-12	Rom 6	Col 2	Luke 12	Ruth 1	1 Cor 13
Eph. 1	Rom 7	Col 3	Luke 13-14	Ruth 2	1 Cor 14-15
Eph. 2	Rom 8	Col 4	Luke 15	Eccl 1	1 Cor 16
Eph. 3	Rom 9	1 Thes 1	Luke 16	Eccl 2	James 1-2
Eph. 4	Rom 10	1 Thes 2	Luke 17-18	Eccl 3	James 3-4
Eph. 5	Rom 11	1 Thes 3	Luke 19-20	Eccl 4	James 5
Eph. 6	Rom 12	1 Thes 4	Luke 21	Eccl 5	James 6
Proverbs 1	Rom 13	1 Thes 5	Luke 22-23	Eccl 6	2 Pet 1-2
Proverbs 2	Rom 14	James 1-2	Luke 24	Eccl 7	2 Pet 3-4
Provebs 3	Rom 15	James 3-4	John 1-3	Eccl 8	2 Cor 1-2
Proverbs 4	Rom 16	James 5	John 4-6	Eccl 9	2 Cor 3-4
Proverbs 5	1 Pet 1	James 6	John 7-9	Eccl 10	2 Cor 5-6
Proverbs 6	1 Pet 2	2 Pet 1	John 10	Eccl 11	2 Cor 7-8
Proverbs 7	1 Pet 3	2 Pet 2	John 11-13	Eccl 12	2 Cor 9-10
Proverbs 8	1 Pet 4	2 Pet 3	John 14-16	James 1	2 Cor 11-12
Proverbs 9	1 Pet 5	Jude 1	John 17	James 2	2 Cor 13

OR MAKE YOUR OWN PLAN

Day 1_____

Day 2_____

Day 3_____

Day 4_____

Day 5_____

Day 6_____

Day 7_____

Day 8_____

Day 9_____

Day 10_____

Day 11_____

Day 12_____

Day 13_____

Day 14_____

Day 15_____

Day 16_____

Day 17_____

Day 18_____

Day 19_____

Day 20_____

Day 21_____

Bible Study Plan Ideas

PLAN 7	PLAN 8	PLAN 9	PLAN 10	PLAN 11	PLAN 12
Proverbs 1	Matthew 1-2	John 1	Acts 1-2	Hebrews 1-2	Job 1-3
Proverbs 2-3	Matthew 3-4	John 2	Acts 3-4	Hebrews 3-5	Job 3-5
Proverbs 4-5	Matthew 5-7	John 3	Acts 5-6	Hebrews 6	Job 6-8
Proverbs 6-7	Matthew 8-10	John 4	Acts 7-8	Hebrews 7-9	Job 9-10
Proverbs 8-9	Matthew 14-16	John 5	Acts 9-10	Hebrews 10	Job 11-13
Proverbs 10	Matthew 17-20	John 6	Acts 11-12	Hebrews 11	Job 14-16
Proverbs 11	Matthew 21-23	John 7	Acts 13-14	Hebrews 12	Job 17-19
Proverbs 12	Matthew 24-26	John 8	Acts 15-16	Hebrews 13	Job 20-22
Proverbs 13	Matthew 27	John 9	Acts 17-18	Psalm 9	Job 23-25
Proverbs 14	Psalm 2	John10	Acts 19-20	Psalm 16	Job 26-27
Proverbs 15	Psalm 8	John 11	Acts 21-22	Psalm 20	Job 28-30
Proverbs 16	Psalm 18	John 12-13	Acts 23-24	Psalm 27	Job 31-33
Proverbs 17	Psalm 22	John 14-15	Acts 25-26	Psalm 29	Job 34-36
Proverbs 18	Psalm 40	John 16-17	Acts 27-28	Psalm 30	Job 37-39
Proverbs 19	Psalm 45	John 18-19	Gal 1	Psalm 34	Job 40
Proverbs 20	Psalm 69	John 20-21	Gal 2	Psalm 37	Job 41-42
Proverbs 21	Psalm 78	1 John 1-2	Gal 3	Psalm 46	Nehemiah 1-3
Proverbs 22	Psalm 89	1 John 3	Gal 4	Psalm 55	Nehemiah 4-6
Proverbs 23	Psalm 110	1 John 4-5	Gal 5	Psalm 147	Nehemiah 7-9
Proverbs 24	Psalm 118	2 John 1	Gal 6	Psalm 107	Nehemiah 10
Proverbs 25	Psalm 119	3 John 1	Psalm 123	Psalm 100	Nehemiah 12-13

OR MAKE YOUR OWN PLAN

Day 1_____	Day 8_____	Day 15_____
Day 2_____	Day 9_____	Day 16_____
Day 3_____	Day 10_____	Day 17_____
Day 4_____	Day 11_____	Day 18_____
Day 5_____	Day 12_____	Day 19_____
Day 6_____	Day 13_____	Day 20_____
Day 7_____	Day 14_____	Day 21_____

Suggested Prayer Topic Ideas & Bible Verses

TEACH ME TO PRAISE AND WORSHIP YOU LORD
Psalm 95:6, 1 Chronicles 16:34, John 4:24, Psalm 13:5-6, Psalm 71:23, Acts 2:46-47, Psalm 149:3.

I AM NOT ALONE
Heb. 13:5, Phil. 4:19, Matt. 7:7, 1 John 1:9, John 14:3.

PREPARING YOUR HEART
Matthew 5:6, Romans 12:1, 2, 1 John 1:9, 3:21-22, John 14:21, Ephesians 5:18, 1 John 5:14-15, 1 Corinthians 12:13, James 4:7; I John 1:9, Titus 3:5.

TRUST IN GOD'S DIVINE GUIDANCE
Jeremiah 29:11, Isaiah 30:21, Isaiah 58:11, Luke 1:7-9, James 1:5-6, Psalm 25:4-5, John 10:27, Ephesians 5:1, Proverbs 3:5-6, Proverbs 1:5, Leviticus 19:31, John 14:26.

SPIRITUAL GIFTS OF GOD
John 3:16, 1 Corinthians 12:4–5, 1 Pet. 4:10, Romans 12:4–6, Ephesians 4:11, Romans 12:8, 1 Corinthians 12:8–10, 1 Corinthians 12:9,28,30, 1 Peter 4:9,10, Romans 12:7, Cor. 12:10, 14:27-28.

SPIRITUAL HUNGER
Matthew 5:6, Psalm 81:10, Deuteronomy 8:3, Isaiah 55:1, John 6:33-35, Psalm 63:1, Psalm 143:6, John 4:13-14, Psalm 42:2, John 7:37.

STRUGGLE WITH GRIEF AND PAIN
Ecclesiastes 11:10, Isaiah 53:4-5.

TEMPTATION
James 4:7, 1 Peter 1:13, 1 Peter 4:7, Job 1:6.

CALM MY ANXIOUS MIND
Philippians 4:6, John 14:27, Isaiah 41:10, Psalm 94:19, Psalm 34:4.

OVERCOMING SELF-WORTH & SELF-DOUBT
Ephesians 2:10,Isaiah 64:8 ,Psalm 139:14,Psalm 46:5, 28:7 ,Romans 5:8,Joshua 1:9.,Psalm 143:8,Colossians 2:10,Song of Songs 4:7 ,1 John 5:14,Isaiah 32:17,1 Peter 1:18-19,Psalm 143:7-8

FREE FROM ACCUSATION
Romans 8:1, Romans 5:1, Romans 8:16-17, Romans 8:16-17.

STRUGGLE WITH FEAR, ANXIETY, OR WORRY
Isaiah 43:1, Matthew 11:28-30, Psalm 23:4, Philippians 4:6-7, Psalm 111:10a, Isaiah 41:13, John 20:19.

STRUGGLING WITH GUILT AND SHAME
2 Corinthians 7:10, Isaiah 54:4a, Isaiah 1:18, Romans 8:1-2, 2 Corinthians 7:9-11.

RENEWING OF MY MIND
Romans 12:2, Philippians 2:12-16, Isaiah 26:3, Ephesians 4:23, Philippians 4:8, Colossians 3:1-2, Romans 8:5, Philippians 4:8.

KEEP MY CONSCIENCE CLEAR
Acts 24:16, Acts 23:1, Hebrews 13:18, Romans 2:15, Exodus 20:16, Exodus 23:1, 1 Peter 2:1-12, Psalm 15:3, Psalm 15:3.

RESTORE MY JOY
Psalm 51:12, John 16:20-22, Psalm 30:11, 16:11; Job 42:10

FULL RESTORATION
Galatians 6:1, Hosea 6:1, Isaiah 61:7, 1 Peter 5:10, Zechariah 9:12, Psalm 71:20-21, Acts 3:19-21, 2 Corinthians 13:9-11, Job 42:10.

EXPECT HEALING MIRACLES
Matthew 17:20, Hebrews 11:6, Mark 9:23-24, Acts 16:29-34, Mark 1:40-42, Jeremiah 17:14, Jeremiah 30:17, Mark 11:24, Jeremiah 33:6, Psalms 147:3, Matthew 4:23, James 5:14-16, Isaiah 53:5, Isaiah 53:4-5, 1 Peter 2:24.

LORD, CAST OUT EVERY SPIRIT OF INFIRMITY
Mark 7:25-30, Luke 13:11-13, Isaiah 58:8, Jeremiah 30:17, Isaiah 53:4, 1 John 3:8.

BE THANKFUL & PRACTICE GRATITUDE
1 Thessalonians 5:18, Psalm 100, Psalm 103, Psalm 34:1-6, Job 33:18 Psalm 16:5-6, Lamentations 3:22, Isaiah 3:10, Isaiah 43:19 , Psalm 67:5-7.

Suggested Prayer Topic Ideas & Bible Verses

CONSECRATION "SUPERNATURAL PURGING AND CLEANSING" OF MY SOUL
Joel 2:15-17, Romans 12:1-12, Malachi 3:3, Matthew 3:12.

SEARCH ME, O GOD
Psalm 139:23-24, 26:1-4, 1 Chronicles 29:17.

FORGIVENESS
Isaiah 1:18, Matthew 5:23-24, 6:14-15, Ephesians 4:26-27, Micah 7:18-19, Colossians 1:13-14, 3:13, Mark 11:35, Luke 17:3, 4, Acts 3:19, 1 Corinthians 6:9-11, 1 John 2:1-2, James 5:16.

FORGIVE LIKE JESUS
Genesis 37-50, Luke 15, 2 Samuel 9, John 8, Matthew 18:21-35.

PLEASE, FORGIVE ME LORD!
2 Chronicles 7:14, 30:9b, 1 John 1:9, Mark 1:15, Luke 13:1-5, 15:7, Proverbs 1:23, 28:13, Acts 3:19, Matthew 9:13, Ezekiel 18:32.

FAMILY
Ecclesiastes 4:9-10, Psalm 127, Joshua 24:15, 1 Timothy 5:8, 1 John 4:19, Colossians 3:13, Proverbs 11:29, Acts 16:31, Romans 12:9.

RESTORE YOUR FAMILY RELATIONSHIP
1 John 4:19, 3:11-15, Colossians 3:13, Proverbs 11:29, 20:7, Acts 16:31, Romans 12:9, Timothy 5:4, Deuteronomy 31:8, Hebrews 13:4,5, James 1:27, Malachi 2:10, John 13:34-35, Galatians 3:28, 1 Corinthians 7:3-4.

SPIRITUAL RENEWAL & DIVINE CONNECTION WITH YOUR SPOUSE
Genesis 2:24, Ephesians 5:25, Romans 12:9, Ephesians 5:28-33, Colossians 3:18-21, 1 Corinthians 6:18, Psalm 128:3, 1 Timothy 5:8, Mark 10:9, Proverbs 18:22, 20:6-7.

SALVATION FOR A LOVED ONE
Luke 19:10, 1 Timothy 2:3-4, Isaiah 52:7.

GOD TEACH ME TO HONOR MY PARENTS
Exodus 20:12, Proverbs 6:20, 1:8, 15:20, Colossians 3:18-21, Ephesians 6:1-2.

TO SET BOUNDARIES
Matthew 5:37, James 5:12, Proverbs 3:35, 22:24, 25, 27:6, Galatians1:10, 6:5, 2 Corinthians 6:14, Proverbs 4:23, 9:7, 22:24-25, 2 Corinthians 6:14, 1 Corinthians 5:11, Psalm 26:4-5, Ephesians 5:6, 6:4.

MAKING DECISIONS
Proverbs 3:5-6, 2:6-8, 16:9, Isaiah 46:9-10, 30:21, 58:11, Luke 1:79, Matthew 6:33, 1 Peter 2:13-17, James 3:17, 32:8, Psalm 27:14, 119:105, Jeremiah 29:11, Philippians 4:6, 4:13, John 15:13, Romans 12:2, Deuteronomy 30:9-10, Ecclesiastes 12:13-14.

TRUSTING GOD IN DIFFICULT TIMES
Jeremiah 32:27, Proverbs 19:21, Psalm 34:17-18, 2 Corinthians 1:3, Psalm 94:19, John 14:27, 2 Corinthians 4:16-18, 2 Corinthians 12:9-10, 1 Peter 4:12-13.

GUIDANCE OF THE HOLY SPIRIT
John 14:16-17, 26; 15:26; 20:22; 16:8-14; 1 Corinthians 2:10-15, Matthew 1:18, 3:11, 16-17, 10:20, Isaiah 63:10, Acts 5:3-4, Ephesians 4:30, Acts 8:29, 13:2, Luke 12:12;, John 16:7-18.

FREEDOM OF MATERIALISTIC ATTITUDE
Proverbs 30:8-9, 10:15; 28:22, Matthew 19:23-24, 2 Corinthians 9:8, 2 Thessalonians 3:10, Ecclesiastes 10:19, Acts 8:20, Jeremiah 9:23-24, Mark 8:36-37. Increase My Faith Lord: Romans 2:4, John 4:6, Acts 16:34, 2 Peter 3:9, Luke 15:28, 17:5, Matthew 5:13-16, 17:20, 19:26, Colossians 1:28-29, 4:17.

TEACH ME TO BE VIGILANT
1 Peter 4:7, 5:8-9, 2 Corinthians 10:4–5, Ephesians 2:1–3, 6:10-18, 1 John 4:1-6,10:10, Acts 17:11, 1 Thessalonians 5:21, 1 Timothy 4:1, 2 Corinthians 13:5.

BE VIGILANT IN THE LAST DAYS
2 Timothy 3:1-5, 3:132 Peter 3:3-4, Matthew 24:3-7, 24:36-39, 1 John 2:18, 1 Thessalonians 5:2-3, 2 Peter 3:7-8, 3:10, 2 Thessalonians 2:1-3, 1 Timothy 4:1, Jude 1:17-19.

Suggested Prayer Topic Ideas & Bible Verses

DELIVER ME FROM EVIL
Matthew 6:13, 4:1-11, 17:19-21, 18:20, 28:18-20,
Acts 16:18, Colossians 1:13, Luke 4:41, Mark 1:34, 5:9,
Luke 8:30, 10:17, 18:1; John 14:14, 15:7,
Ephesians 5:18-20, 6:10-18, Colossians 1:20, 3:16-17,
2 Timothy 3:16-17, Hebrews 4:12, James 5:14-16,
1 John 1:9, 4:1-8.

PROTECTION FROM SPIRITUAL ATTACK
1 Peter 4:12-13, Ephesians 6:12, Psalm 141:5,
James 4:7, Deuteronomy 33:27, Genesis 17:1,
Jeremiah 23:24, 32:7, Psalms 6:8-10, 72:12-14.

VICTORY IN SPIRITUAL WARFARE
Mark 16:17, Luke 9:1-2, 10:17-20, Revelation 3:5,
12:7-11, 20:7-15, 21:7, Matthew 25:41, Romans 8:15,37,
1 Corinthians 15:57, 1 Chronicles 29:11,
1 John 5:4, Hebrews 2:14-15.

ASSURANCE OF SALVATION
John 3:16, 5:24, 6:37, 44, 10:28-29, Romans 8:1,
Ephesians 1:13-14, Colossians 1:12-14, 1 Peter 1:3-4;
1 John 2:1-2; 5:13.

REJECTION OF IMMORALITY
2 Corinthians 7:1, Titus 2:11-14, 2 Tim 2:21,
Matthew 5:27-32, 19:9, 1 Corinthians 6:9-10, 18-20,
Hebrews 13:4, Exodus 20,14, Deuteronomy 5:18, 24:1-4,
Luke 18:20, James 2:11, 2 Peter 2:14, 1 Corinthians 5:9,
Ephesians 5:3, Leviticus 20:10, I Thessalonians 4:3.

WALK IN INTEGRITY
Proverbs 2:6-8, 4:25-27, 10:9, 11:3, 12:22, 28:6, 2
Corinthians 8:21, Hebrews 13:18, 2 Samuel 22:26,
Psalm 25:19-21, 101:2, Psalm 119:1, Titus 2:7-8.

NO MORE MURMURING & COMPLAINING
1 Corinthians 10:10-11, 1 Peter 4:9, 1 Timothy 2:8,
Colossians 3:8, Ephesians 4:29, Exodus 16:7, James 5:9.

SPIRITUAL TRANSFORMATION
2 Corinthians 4:8, 16, 5:17, Colossians 3:1-17,
Philippians 1:6, John 17:17, Romans 6:11, 8:5.

FINANCIAL BREAKTHROUGH CAREER, BUSINESS
Proverbs 10:4, 18:16, 22:29, 10:4, Daniel 6:3-4,
Psalms 5:12, Luke 2:52, Genesis 26:22.

SPIRITUAL GIFTS OF GOD
John 3:16, 1 Peter 4:10, 14:27-28, Romans 12:4–8,
Ephesians 4:11, 1 Corinthians 12:8–10, 28, 30, 14:27-28.

PRAYER FOR THE CHURCH
Acts 2:42- 47, Acts 6:4, 2 Corinthians 7:1, Galatians 6:9.

PRAYER FOR THE THE NATION
Jeremiah 29:7, Psalm 91:4-7, Mark 4:37-39, 7:25-30,
Proverbs 11:14, 14:34, 19:21, 1 Timothy 2:1-2,
Isaiah 53:4, 5, 1 Peter 2:24.

CONFLICT RESOLUTION
Matthew 18:15-17, Proverbs 15:1, 20:18, 1 Peter 3:8-11,
Ephesians 4:26, Luke 12:51, 16:7, 17:3, Hebrews 12:15,
Romans 12:19.

FASTING FOR SPIRITUAL BREAKTHROUGH
Exodus 34:27-28, Judges 20:26, Esther 4:3, 16,
Nehemiah 1:4, 2 Samuel 1:12, Samuel 31:13, 1
Chronicles 10:12, 1 Kings 19:1-9, Daniel 9:3, 10:1-3,
6:18, Jonah 3:5, Matthew 4:2, Mark 9:29, Acts 14:23,
1 Corinthians 7:5, 11:24-28.

PRAY WITHOUT CEASING
Hebrew 4:16, Matt. 9-10, 7:7, James 5:16, 1:6,
Luke 11:9, 22:41-42, Jeremiah 29:12, 33:3, Romans
12:12, Philippians 4:6-7, Mark 11:24,
Colossians 3:17, 4:2, 1 Thessalonians 5:16-18,
1 John 5:14, 14:13.

OVERCOMING BITTERNESS
Hebrews 12:15, Ephesians 4:31-32, Matt. 6:15, 26:75,
Luke 22:62, Acts 8:23, Rom. 3:14, Eph. 4:31, James 3:11,
14, Proverbs 17:25, Lamentations 1:4, Amos 8:10,
Ezekiel. 27:30, Isaiah 33:7, 2 Kings 14:26, Job 7:11, 10:1,
Deuteronomy 32:24, Acts 8:23, Colossians 3:19,
Proverbs 14:10, Jeremiah 2:1, Job 9:17-18.

Suggested Prayer Topic Ideas & Bible Verses

OVERCOMING WRONG THOUGHTS
2 Corinthians 10:5, Psalm 139:23-24, 141:3-4,
Isaiah 26:3-4, Romans 12:2, Ephesians 4:22-24,
Philippians 3:18-21.

BREAKING FREE FROM ANGER
Ephesians 4:26, 4:31-32, Proverbs 15:1, Romans 12:19,
Proverbs 14:29, Proverbs 29:11, Romans 12:21,
Ephesians 4:26-27, James 1:19-20, Proverbs 30:33,
Ephesians 4:30-31, Philippians 4:5.

SUPPORT OF MY FAMILY & FRIENDS
Romans 12:4-5, Psalms 127:1-5 , 133:1 ,Philippians
2:4,Galatians 6:2, 1 Thessalonians 5:11 ,Hebrews
10:24-25, 1 Peter 4:10,Matthew 18:20 ,Proverbs 27:17.

TAKE CARE OF YOUR BODY
Matthew 6:27, 1 Timothy 4:8, Ephesians 5:29,
1 Corinthians 3:17, 6:19-20, 8:9, Proverbs 4:23,
1 Corinthians 6:20.

UNITY
Mathew 12:25, 1 Peter3:8, 1 John 4:11, Philippians 2:2,
1 Corinthians 1:10, Romans 14:19, Colossians 3:15-17,
Acts 20:28, Hebrews 10:24, John 15:13.

FALLING IN LOVE WITH GOD
Matthew 7:11, 22:36-40, Romans 8:28, Proverbs 4:23,
Deuteronomy 6:6, John 10:28, 14:21, 2 Chronicles 16:9,
Revelation 2:4, Hebrews 13:5.

TO BE CONTENT
Philippians 4:11-13, Matthew 6:25-26,
Hebrews 13:5,Hebrews 13:5,1-timothy 6:6-7,
1-Timothy 6:10-11, Proverbs 15: 13, 16:8,28:6, 30:7-9,
Ecclesiastes 3:13, 2Timothy6:6, James 4:1-10, Proverbs
14:30, Deuteronomy 6:5, 1 Peter 5:6-7,Matthew 6:33
,Romans 8:28, 1 Peter 3:3-4, Ecclesiastes 6:9, Luke
12:15 ,2 Corinthians 12:10 ,Luke 3:14 ,1 Timothy 6:8 .

PRAY FOR THE PEACE OF JERUSALEM
Romans 10:1, Psalm 122:6, 89:28-37, Genesis 12:2-3,
1 John 3:18, Luke 7:1-5, 19:41, Duet. 6:3-4, 32:10,
Zech. 2:8,Numb. 24:9, Malachi 3:6, Ephesians 2:19,
Romans 11:17-24.

SPIRITUAL CLEANSE
Deuteronomy 6:5-7, 7:26, Psalm 51, Leviticus 19:31,
20:6-7, 27, Exodus 20:27, 22:18, Deuteronomy 7:26,
18:10-12, 1 Chronicles 10:13-14, Isaiah 8:19-20,
Galatians 5:20, Revelation 21:8,

WISDOM
James 3:17, James 1:5, Proverbs 3:13-18,
Proverbs 17:27-28, Colossians 2:8, Psalm 19:7.

CALM MY ANXIOUS MIND
Philippians 4:6, John 14:27, Isaiah 41:10,
Psalm 94:19, Psalm 34:4.

FREEDOM FROM FEAR
Psalm 56:3, 1 Peter 5:7. 2 Corinthians 12:10,
Philippians 4:13.

PERSEVERANCE
2 Thessalonians 3:13, James 1:2-4, 1 Peter 5:7,
John 15:7, 2 Peter 1:10

EXPECT MIRACLES
Matthew 8:14-15, 26-27; 9:2, 6-7, 27-30; Mark 1:32-34;
John 2:1-11; 6:10-14; John 10:24-25; 20:30-31; 3:2

TO BE A GODLY WIFE
Mark 10:6-9, Matthew 19:4-6, Titus 2:4-5, Acts 10:2,
1 Timothy 3:11, Ephesians 4:2,1,5: 22-33, 5:21,
1 Peter 3:1-7, Esther 1:20,1 Corinthians 11:3 ,
Deuteronomy 5:18, 1 Corinthians 13:4-8,
Proverbs 11:29 , 12:4 , 14:1, 18: 22, 19:14, 25:24 ,
31:10-31, 1 Peter 4:8, Hebrews 13:4.

TO BE A GODLY HUSBAND
Genesis 1:27, Genesis 2:23-24, Mt 19:4, 5,
Ephesians 3 :14-15, 4:12, 5:21-32 ,28, 1 Peter 5:5,
2 Peter 1:21, Galatians 6:2, 1 Corinthians 3:2, 7:3-5,
6:11, 11:13 , 13:13, Romans 12:1-2, Hebrews 5:12; 6:1,
13:4, Job 31:1, Job 31:1, Corinthians 7:2,, 11:1,
Hebrews 13:4, 1 Timothy 3:12 ,2 Timothy 1:13,
Psalm 51 , 119:37, 128:3, Galatians 5:13, 6:1,
Colossians 1:22, 3:16-19, Exodus 20:14, James 3:13-18 ,
4:6, 5:20, Proverbs 5:18, Philippians 2:5-8, John
3:3;-53:5; Matthew 5:19, 28, 20:24-28;23:12
Mark 10:41-45; Luke 16:18 ,22:24-27.

Prayer Calendar

Date: _____ to _____

SUNDAY	MONDAY	TUESDAY	WEDNESDAY
GOD OF OPEN DOORS "Here I am! I stand at the door and knock. If anyone hears my voice and opens the door, I will come in and eat with that person, and they with me." *-Revelation 3:20*	**I AM NOT ALONE** "Never Will I Leave You; Never Will I Forsake You." *-Hebrews 13:5*	**SEEK GOD FIRST** "You will seek me and find me when you seek me with all your heart." *-Jeremiah 29:13*	**DO NOT DWELL ON THE PAST** "Forget the former things; do not dwell on the past" *-Isaiah 43:18*
REJECT & RECOGNIZE FALSE THOUGHTS "We demolish arguments and every pretension that sets itself up against the knowledge of God, and we take captive every thought to make it obedient to Christ." *-2 Corinthians 10:5*	**RENEW YOUR MIND** "Be transformed by the renewing of your mind" *Romans 12:2*	**HUMBLE MIND** "Humble yourselves, therefore, under God's mighty hand, that he may lift you up in due time. Cast all your anxiety on him because he cares for you. Renewing of the mind". *1 Peter 5:6,7*	**BE ACCOUNTABLE** Gives us power, love and self-discipline " *-2 Timothy 1:7*
GUARD THE HEART "Above all else, guard your heart, for everything you do flows from it." *-Proverbs 4:23*	**PRAYING IN THE HOLY SPIRIT** "But you, dear friends, by building yourselves up in your most holy faith and praying in the Holy Spirit. *-Jude 1:10*	**PROVISION** "Do not be anxious, saying, 'What shall we eat?' or 'What shall we drink?' or 'What shall we wear?' For the Gentiles seek after all these things, and your heavenly Father knows that you need them all. But seek first the kingdom of God and his righteousness, and all these things will be added to you. *-Matt. 6:31–33*	**CALM MY ANXIOUS MIND** "So do not fear, for I am with you do not be dismayed, for I am your God. I will strengthen you and help you I will uphold you with my righteous right hand." *-Isaiah 41:10*
CONFESS If we confess our sins, He is faithful and just to forgive us our sins and to cleanse us from all unrighteousness." *-1 John 1:9*	**SPIRITUAL HUNGER** "Create in me a pure heart, O God, and renew a steadfast spirit within me. Do not cast me from your presence or take your Holy Spirit from me. Restore to me the joy of my salvation and grant me a willing spirit, to sustain me." *-Psalm 51:10-12*	**ASK FOR WISDOM** "I keep asking that the God of our Lord Jesus Christ, the glorious Father, may give you the Spirit of wisdom and revelation, so that you may know him better. I pray also that the eyes of your heart may be enlightened in order that you may know the hope to which he has called you, the riches of his glorious inheritance in the saints, and the incomparably great power for us who believe. *-Ephesians 1:17-18*	**BE FRUITFUL** "But the fruit of the Spirit is love, joy, peace, patience, kindness, goodness, faithfulness, gentleness and self-control." *-Galatians 5:22*

Prayer Calendar

Date: _____ to _____

THURSDAY	FRIDAY	SATURDAY	NOTES
REST IN GOD "Come to me, all who labor and are heavy laden, and I will give you rest. Take my yoke upon you, and learn from me, for I am gentle and lowly in heart, and you will find rest for your souls. For my yoke is easy, and my burden is light." -Matt. 11:28–30	**JOY AND PEACE** "May the God of hope fill you with all joy and peace as you trust in him, so that you may overflow with hope by the power of the Holy Spirit." -Romans 15:13	**THE ARMOR OF GOD** Put on the full armor of God, so that you can take your stand against the devil's schemes. For our struggle is not against flesh & blood, but against the rulers against the authorities, against the powers of this dark world and against the spiritual forces of evil in the heavenly realms. -Ephesians 6:10-20	
DO NOT FEAR "Say to those with fearful hearts, "Be strong, do not fear; your God will come, he will come with vengeance; with divine retribution he will come to save you." -Isaiah 35:4	**BE REAL** "Love must be sincere. Hate what is evil; cling to what is good. -Romans 12:9	**FORGIVE** "Bear with each other & forgive one another if any of you has a grievance against someone. Forgive as the Lord forgave you." -Colossians 3:13	
BE VIGILANT "But examine everything carefully; hold fast to that which is good." -Thessalonians 5:21	**PROTECTION** "The Lord will keep you from all harm- he will watch over your life; the Lord will watch over your coming and going both now and forevermore." -Psalm 121:8	**SPIRITUAL PROTECTION** "But the Lord is faithful, and he will strengthen you and protect you from the evil one." -2 Thessalonians 3:3	
PRACTICE GRATITUDE "Let the peace of Christ rule in your hearts, since as members of one body you were called to peace. And be thankful." -Colossians 3:15	**PRAY** "Rejoice in hope, be patient in tribulation, be constant in prayer." -Romans 12:10	**BELIEVE** "If you believe, you will receive whatever you ask for in prayer." -Matthew 21:22	

PRAYERS WITH DECREES & DECLARATIONS FOR BREAKTHROUGHS, OVERCOMING, AND RESTORATION

"The reality is, my prayers don't change God. But, I am convinced prayer changes me. Praying boldly boots me out of that stale place of religious habit into authentic connection with God Himself." - Lysa TerKeurst

RENEWING YOUR COMMITMENT (THE CREED)

I believe in God the Father, Creator of heaven and earth, who sent His only begotten Son because of His love for us. I believe in Jesus Christ, my personal Lord and Savior who came to the world and became flesh. I believe in the power of His death and resurrection that brought forth my salvation. By His stripes, I was healed of my transgressions and by his blood I was forgiven of all my sins. I have been crucified with Christ. Therefore, it is no longer I who live, but Christ within me. I am confident that I will live a life in eternity because Jesus overcame death. I am victorious, and I am conqueror because of Jesus' victory. I believe in the Holy Spirit, whom the Father has sent to be His advocate and my guide. I renew my covenant with the Godhead today, acknowledging that God is one in three persons – the Father, the Son, and the Holy Spirit. I vow to be a faithful servant of God today, tomorrow, and for all eternity, in Jesus' Name.

Suggested verses: John 3:16, John 1:14, Isaiah 53:5, Romans 10:9-10, 1 Corinthians 15:55-57, Galatians 2:20, Romans 8:37, John 14:26, Deuteronomy 4:6, 1 John 5:7.

PLEAD THE BLOOD OF JESUS

I plead, the blood of Jesus against Satan and declare that I am an overcomer by the blood of the Lamb, I plead the blood of Jesus against deadly pestilence, I plead the blood of Jesus against the terror of night, I plead the blood of Jesus and confess by faith that the angel of death passes over my house, I plead the blood of Jesus against every smiting disease and attack of the enemy, I plead the blood of Jesus against any mental, spiritual and physical imprisonment in the name of Jesus, I plead the blood of Jesus and declare that throughout this year I will stand under the blood and Satan cannot touch me, in Jesus' Name.

Suggested verses: 1 Peter 1:18-19, 1 John 1:7, Hebrews 9:14, Revelation 1:5, Romans 3:24-25, Ephesians 1:7.

REJECT SATANIC ASSOCIATION AND SUGGESTION

I reject my former life of living in drunkenness, promiscuousness and all forms of godlessness. I confess that I am a new creation, the old things in my life have gone and the new have come. I am a redeemed child of the Lord; washed by the blood of the Lamb, and saved by His grace, I reject a life of strife and envy in the name of Jesus, I reject any relationship that may drag me into ungodly habits in Jesus name, I reject the sins of the mouth, sensual sins, malice, and hypocrisy in the name of Jesus, I reject Satan's suggestion that I will not achieve success and confess that in this very year of restoration, I shall walk from minimum to maximum in the name of Jesus.

Suggested verses: 2 Corinthians 5:17, Ephesians 1:7, Ephesians 2:8, 1 Thessalonians 5:22-23, Psalm 23:3.

DESTROY ALL NEGATIVE PRONOUNCEMENTS

I destroy all powers that expand problems, and pray they shall be paralyzed in the name of Jesus, I destroy every yoke of Satan coming my way and every evil pronouncement of the wicked people around me in the name of Jesus, I destroy every ungodly covenant I might have been enticed to make in the name the Lord Jesus. I destroy the curses of Baalams around me in the name of Jesus, I destroy the power of agent of debt in my life in the name of Jesus, I destroy the power of the agent of spiritual rags in my life in the name of Jesus, I destroy all the lies of the enemy that say I cannot make it in this year in Jesus name, I destroy every trait of spiritual backwardness in Jesus' Name.

Suggested verses: Ephesians 6:12, Mark 16:17, Galatians 3:13-14, Galatians 5:1, 2 Timothy 4:18, Psalm 34:17, Isaiah 54:17.

• I declare God is working all things together for my good. He has a master plan for my life. He knows the plans that he has for me, plans to prosper me and not to harm me, plans to give me hope and a future. And in his perfect time, everything will come together and it'll all make sense.
Suggested verses: Romans 8:28, Jeremiah 29:11, Habakkuk 2:3.

REPOSSESS YOUR TERRITORIES

I repossess the land that I have lost, in the name of the Lord, I repossess supernatural financing to rebuild every broken place, I repossess and inhabit every possession stolen from me, I repossess my job, my health, my business, my marriage in Jesus name, I repossess my financial break-throughs. I retrieve my blessings from the evil confiscators, in the name of Jesus, I repossess my victory. I confess that I am delivered from the power of darkness. My battles belong to the Lord; he will fight all my battles throughout this year and I will triumph over my enemies in the name of the Lord, I repossess my vision. I confess that abundance of new ideas and favors are mine in the name of Jesus.

Suggested verses: Deuteronomy 30:3-13, Exodus 14:14, Zechariah 4:6, 2 Chronicles 20:15, Psalm 44:5.

CONFESS RESTORATION IN YOUR LIFE

I confess, that all my brokenness shall be mended by the Lord in this very year in Jesus name, I confess that the Spirit of Confusion shall not have power over me and my household. The Lord will teach me and instruct me the way I should go; he will counsel me and watch over me, I confess that Satan will not rule over me; I break the power of sin over me. I am free from the oppression of the power of darkness. The blood of Jesus has set me free, I confess that my light shall shine brightly in the name of Jesus, I confess that the lamp of the wicked around me shall be snuffed out in the name of Jesus, I confess that I shall be restored spiritually, emotionally, socially, physically, financially, mentally, and matrimonially in Jesus name, I confess that all who rage against me will surely be ashamed and disgraced, I confess that all who oppose my restoration, breakthroughs and victory will be as nothing & perish, I confess that the Lord will go before me throughout this year; he will level the mountains; he will break down gates of bronzes and cut through bars of iron. The Lord will give me treasures now hidden, and riches that are stored in secret places, in Jesus' Name.

Suggested verses: Isaiah 54, Joel 2:25 - 2:26, Psalm 23:5, Romans 10:11, Isaiah 45:2-3.

CALL FORTH YOUR LOST AND STOLEN BREAKTHROUGHS

I call forth all my treasures that the enemy has stolen, I receive them in this very year of restoration in the name of Jesus, I call forth the blessings of the Lord on all my projects in this year. There shall be no abandon projects, time and life wasting projects on my way in this year in Jesus name, I call forth the anointing for creativity in my business and my ministry to fall on me powerfully in Jesus name, I call forth my lost and stolen financial breakthrough in Jesus name, I call forth an accelerating breakthrough on my way this year in Jesus name, I call forth prosperity around my home in Jesus name, I call forth divine wisdom and understanding that bring about success in Jesus name, I call forth shattered dreams shattered hope be revived and achievable for me in Jesus name, I call forth the spirit of watchfulness and spiritual alertness in Jesus name.

Suggested verses: 1 Samuel 30: 1-8, 18-19, Isaiah 58:11-12, Job 42:10, Joel 2:25, Deuteronomy 30:3-13.

RECEIVE YOUR SPIRITUAL COMPASS

I receive the Name of the Lord as my strong tower, I run into it and I am safe, I receive the Word of the Lord as the lamp unto my feet. No darkness shall come my way throughout this year in the name of the Lord, I receive faith in the Lord, mountains shall crumble before me this year, I receive the grace of the Lord, therefore, special favor will come to me from the East, from West, from the North and from the South in Jesus name, I receive the Presence of the Almighty God with me at all times this year, therefore, Goliaths will fall before me, I receive the Jericho-wall-destroying-power, therefore, every stone of hindrance, shall be rolled out of my way, in Jesus name, I receive patience, therefore, I will not run ahead of God on every issue of my life. I receive wisdom from above, therefore, I will manage my affairs as the Lord wants me to in the name of Jesus.

Suggested verses: Proverbs 18:10, Psalm 119:105, 1 John 1:5, Joshua 6:2-3; 20-21.

THANK HIM FOR HIS BENEFITS

I thank the Lord for giving me the privilege to see this season of restoration, breakthroughs, overcoming and conquering, I thank the Name of the Lord for keeping me and my household safe throughout this past year, I thank Him for giving me good health, I thank Him for giving me victory, I thank Him for healing me, I thank Him for sheltering me, I thank Him for forgiving me, I thank Him for favoring me, I thank Him for saving me, in Jesus' Name.

Suggested verses: Psalm 28: 6-7, Psalm 34:1-3, Psalm 103, 1 Kings 8:56, Luke 1:68, Ephesians 1:3, Daniel 2:20.

BLESS HIM FOR FAVOR

I believe that in this year of restoration, I will break down all strongholds keeping me from my blessings in the name of Jesus Christ of Nazareth, I believe that my mouth shall be filled with laughter, I believe that my tongue shall sing songs of joy, I believe that the Lord will do great and mighty things in my life in this very year of restoration in the name of Jesus, I believe that the Lord will restore my fortunes and all that I have sowed with tears; I shall reap with songs of joy, in the name of Jesus, I believe that all my years of fruitlessness will be transformed into fruitfulness, with a mighty harvest in the name of Jesus, I believe that greater is He that dwells in me; the Lord will do greater things in my life in this year in the name of the Lord, I believe that throughout this year, my family and I will dwell in the secret place of the most High God. We will rest in the shadow of the Almighty, I believe that the Lord is my refuge and my fortress, I believe that the Lord will save me from the fowler's snare and from the deadly pestilence, I believe that the Lord will cover me with his feathers and that under his wings I will find refuge in the name of Jesus.

Suggested verses: Psalm 126, 1 John 4:4, 1 Samuel 12:16, Psalm 91.

PROPHESY YOUR DESTINY

I declare I will experience God's faithfulness. I will not worry. I will not doubt. I will keep on trusting in God's unfailing love. I receive every promise that God has spoken over me, and I will become everything that God created me to be. I will see an explosion of God's goodness, a sudden widespread of increase. I will experience the surpassing greatness of God's favor and it will take me into a higher level of faith and spiritual maturity. Explosive blessings are coming my way. I declare I have the grace I need for today. I am full of power, strength, and determination. Nothing I will face will be too much for me because I am made to outlast the storm. I declare God's perfect timing in my life. I have not missed my window of opportunity. God has moments of favor in my future. Everything that I have experienced is preparing me for the great calling that God has placed in my life. This is my time. This is my moment, I receive it today!

Suggested verses: 2 Thessalonians 3:3, Philippians 4:6-7, Psalm 13:5, Psalm 27:13, 2 Corinthians 12:9,
2 Timothy 1:7, Philippians 4:13, Ecclesiastes 3:11, Jeremiah 29:11.

PRAY FOR PERFECT HEALTH

I pray that throughout this year I shall enjoy the favor of God's covenant Name of Jehovah Rapha, I pray, by the stripes of Jesus I have been healed. My body is strong in Jesus name, I pray that no weapon that is fashioned against me shall prosper in Jesus name, I pray that every agent of infirmity must lose its hold over my life in the name of Jesus, I pray against any sickness or disease that the enemy may want to use to stop my destiny in Jesus name, I pray against every genetic disease that has ruled my family for generations in Jesus name, I pray against every form of torment, whether physical or spiritual in Jesus name, I pray that the anointing of God will flow from my life to bring healing, deliverance and hope to others in the name of Jesus, I pray that throughout this year every member of my household will receive the healing of the Lord, in Jesus' Name.

Suggested verses: Exodus 23:25, 1 Peter 2:24, Isaiah 53:5, Isaiah 54:17.

DECLARE ABUNDANCE

I declare by faith that Jesus will supply all my needs, spiritually, financially, physically and emotionally throughout this year, I declare that every aspect of my life will yield abundant fruit in Jesus name, I declare that I shall be a blessing to the people of God and the work of God, I declare that God will enrich my life with the abundance of His joy, I declare that God will shower me with such an abundance of His favor that even the enemy will have to acknowledge it in Jesus name, I declare that I shall be blessed with supernatural abundance that will bless generations to come in Jesus name, I declare that the power, glory and the kingdom of the living God will come upon every aspect of my life, in the name of Jesus.

Suggested verses: Philippians 4:19, Genesis 12:1-3, Ephesians 3:20, Psalm 65:11, Proverbs 3:10, Deuteronomy 28:12.

• I declare that I am blessed with good health, a happy family, great friends, and long life. I am happy and contented with what I have at the moment. And as I count my blessings each day I realize that I have more than enough. I declare that I will lend and not borrow, and I will be above and not beneath.
Suggested verses: Deuteronomy 15:6, 2 Corinthians 9:8.

BIND ALL FORCES WARRING AGAINST YOUR HOME

I bind every power of darkness that opposes my restoration in this year in the name of Jesus, I bind all the evil hosts that may want to gather against my progress, and against my family in the name of Jesus, I bind all the spirits of rebellion around all my children in Jesus name, I bind the spirit of laziness in any form in my life and my family in the name of the Lord, I bind the spirit of dryness, barrenness, and backwardness in my home in the name of the Lord Jesus Christ.

Suggested verses: Joshua 24:15, Isaiah 54:17, Romans 15:5, 1 Corinthians 1:10, Deuteronomy 7:14, Psalm 91.

DECREE GOD'S BLESSINGS ON YOUR CHILDREN

I decree the blessings of God over every plan and goal for my children in this year, I decree all my children shall be taught of the Lord, I decree my children shall be for signs and wonders. They shall walk in obedience, I decree that every promise of the Lord concerning my children will not fall to the ground but each shall be literally fulfilled in Jesus name, I decree that my children will have personal intimate relationship with God, and the fear of the Lord will be evident in their daily walk with God, I decree in Jesus name that my children would not be a source of affliction but a testimony to God's grace, I decree none of my children will bring shame to the name of the Lord, I decree that no generational curse shall have any effect upon my children in Jesus name.

Suggested verses: Genesis 17:7-8, Psalm 112:2, Psalm 103:17-18, Proverbs 20:7, Proverbs 11:21,
Isaiah 54:13, Galatians 3:13.

COMMAND THE ENEMY TO LEAVE YOUR MARRIAGE

I command, that all anti-testimony forces working against my marriage will scatter into irreparable pieces, in the name of Jesus. I command that the fire of God be sent into the camp of those gathering to do harm to my marriage and my possessions. I command all powers and principalities to take their hands off my marriage and everything that belongs to me in Jesus name. I command the collapse of every stronghold and towerof Babel before my marriage in this very year in the name of Jesus. I command that every activity that does not promote the design of God for my marriage in this year to collapse in the name of the Lord. I command that mountains of impossibilities that are facing my marriage to fall in this year of restoration in the name of Jesus.

Suggested verses: Mark 10:9, Matthew 19:6, Ecclesiastes 4:12, 1 Corinthians 10:13, 2 Corinthians 10:5.

RELEASE BLESSINGS UNTO YOUR CHURCH

I release growth into my Church. May the fire of evangelism be burning in the heart of every member of my Church in the name of Jesus, I release fresh anointing upon the ministry of my Church. May the Lord clothe my pastor with a double portion of His anointing, I release the spirit that desirs for corporate prayer, fasting and studying of the Word of God into my Church in Jesus name, I release the love of God that covers a multitude of sins into my Church. I call forth the spirit of forgiveness into the life of every member of my Church in the name of Jesus, I release favor, integrity, humility, and purity into the life of the assistant pastor. May the Lord cover him and his entire family with the blood of Jesus, I release signs and wonders to back up the messages from my Pastor in the name of Jesus, I release into my Church, special open doors for the proclamation of the Word, in Jesus name.

Suggested verses: 1 Corinthians 12:12-31, Ephesians 4:11-16, Isaiah 33:20-24, Isaiah 61:7, Hebrews 2:3-4,
Acts 14:3, 1 Timothy 5:17, Hebrews 13:17, 1 Thessalonians 5:12-13.

DECLARE AN OUTPOURING OF GOD'S SPIRIT

I decree and declare an outpouring of God's Spirit as promised in the book of Joel. I declare a great revival in all the churches. In Jesus' Name, I break the yoke of ungodliness, religiosity, and idolatry. I release a fresh anointing over the pastor and all the church leaders, that they may become a catalyst for revival. I break the barrenness of all the churches worldwide and I pray for a birth of multitudes of God's people serving in the church with zeal and passion in Jesus' Name. I also declare that God will raise up missionaries that He can send to the ends of the earth to spread the gospel. May God's vision for the world and for His Church come to pass and not be hindered by any principality, in Jesus' name.

Suggested verses: Joel 2:28, Acts 1:8, Acts 2:17, Isaiah 44:3, Isaiah 52:7.

RELEASE BLESSINGS UNTO YOUR NATION

I release blessings over my beloved country. May the Holy Spirit envelope the whole nation, including every state, every province, every town and municipality. I pray that all my fellowmen will come to know the saving power of Jesus Christ. I speak of salvation in every corner of each household. May the Lord bless every family living in my country and keep them safe from any calamities or danger in Jesus' Name. I lift up all the government officials in every branch of the government- executive, legislative, and judiciary. I declare wisdom, discernment, honesty, and integrity to be upon them as they make major decisions for our country. I bless the president and I call forth God's army of angels to surround him all the time. I cancel all the schemes of the enemy over his life in Jesus' Name. I pray that God will send godly people to counsel and disciple him. I speak of salvation to all the government officials and their families. I bind all the principalities surrounding our nation and I release the spirit of unity, prosperity, and abundance in Jesus' Name.

Suggested verses: Genesis 12:2, 2 Chronicles 7:14, I Timothy 2:1-2, Romans 13:1, Proverbs 11:14.

EVERYDAY AFFIRMATIONS AND DECLARATIONS

• I declare that I am grateful for what God has done in my life. I will not take for granted the people, opportunities and favor he has blessed me with. I will thank God for what I have and not complain about what I don't have. I will consider each day as a gift from God. My heart will praise and thank Him for all His goodness.
Suggested verses: 1 Thessalonians 5:18, Philippians 4:12, Psalm 9:1.

• I declare a legacy of faith over my life and that I will store up blessings for future generations. My life is marked by excellence and integrity. Because I making the right choices and taking steps of faith, others will want to follow me. God's abundance is surrounding my life today.
Suggested verses: Proverbs 13:22, Psalm 32:8.

• I declare that God has a great plan for my life. He is directing my steps. And even though I may not understand what God is doing, I will choose to trust in His great plan. He will work out every detail to my advantage. In his perfect time, everything will turn out right.
Suggested verses: Jeremiah 29:11, Proverbs 3:6, John 13:7, Romans 8:28, Ecclesiastes 3:11.

• I declare that God's dream for my life is coming to pass. It will not be stopped by people, disappointments, or adversities. God has all the solutions for every problem I will be facing. The right people and the right breaks are coming in my future. I will fulfill my destiny.
Suggested verses: Jeremiah 29:11, Psalm 138:8.

• I declare unexpected blessings are coming my way. As God gives the increase, I will all the more humble myself. For those who exalt themselves will be humbled, and those who humble themselves will be exalted.
Suggested verse: Matthew 23:12.

• I am not average! I have been custom made I am one of a kind. Of all the things God created, what He is the most proud of is me. I am his masterpiece, his most prized possession. I'll keep my head held high, knowing I am a child of the Most High God, made in His image and likeness.
Suggested verses: Psalm 139:14, Ephesians 2:10, Galatians 3:26, Galatians 4:7.

• I declare that I will use my words to bless people. I speak favor and victory over my family, friends, and loved ones. I will help call out their seeds of greatness by telling them " I'm proud of you, I love you, you are amazing, you are talented, you are beautiful, you will do great things in life."
Suggested verses: Proverbs 18:21, Matthew 12:36-27, Matthew 15:18, Matthew 12:34.

• I declare that I am calm and peaceful. I will not let people or circumstances upset me. I will remain calm in all situations knowing that God has given me the gift of self-control. I choose to live my life happy, bloom where I am planted, and let God fight my battles.
Suggested verses: 2 Timothy 1:7, John 14:27.

• I declare that I will live as a healer. I am sensitive to the needs of those around me. I was called to spread God's love and comfort the afflicted. I am full of compassion and kindness. I will not just look for a miracle; I will become someone's miracle by showing God's love and mercy everywhere I go. I declare I will put action behind by faith. I will not be passive or indifferent. I demonstrate my faith by acting upon the burden He has placed in my heart.
Suggested verses: Isaiah 61:1, James 2:14-26.

• I declare breakthroughs are coming in my life, sudden bursts of God's goodness. Not a trickle. But a flood of God's favor and power. I am expecting God to overwhelm me with his goodness and mercy.
Suggested verse: Psalm 23:6.

• I declare God's Supernatural favor over my life. For what is impossible for men is possible with God. Supernatural opportunities, supernatural healing, supernatural restoration, and supernatural breakthroughs are coming. I am getting stronger, healthier, and wiser.
Suggested verses: Luke 18:27, Matthew 19:26, Mark 9:23, Jeremiah 32:27.

• I declare that I am a people builder. I will act on every opportunity to help others achieve their dreams. I will speak words of faith and victory, affirming them, proving them, and letting them know they are valued. I will help them to rise higher and become all that God created them to be.
Suggested verses: Matthew 5:16, Matthew 22:39, John 15:12, John 13:34-35.

• I declare that I will speak only positive words of faith and victory, over myself, over my friends, my family and future. I will not use my words to describe the situation. I will use my words to change my situation. I will call in favor, healing, and restoration. I will face any problem with confidence knowing that my God is powerful.
Suggested verses: Proverbs 18:21, Matthew 12:36-27, Matthew 15:18, Matthew 12:34.

• I declare that I will choose faith over fear! I will try my best to focus on the positive side of every situation. I will use my energy not to worry but to believe. Fear has no part in my life. I will not dwell on the negative, discouraging thoughts. My mind is set on what God says about me. Because his plan for me is success, victory, and abundance.
Suggested verses: Mark 5:36, Hebrews 11:6, 2 Corinthians 5:7, Mark 9:23, Joshua 1:9, Psalm 27:1.

• I declare that I am anointed and empowered by the Creator of the universe. Every bondage and every limitation is being broken off of me. This is my time to shine. I will emerge victorious in every situation.
Suggested verses: Isaiah 60:1, 1 John 2:27.

• I declare that God has big things prepared for me. I will pray bold prayers, expect big and believe big I will ask God to align my plans according to His will. I will be patient in waiting for God to answer. I will pray with boldness, with thanksgiving, and without ceasing.
Suggested verses: 1 Corinthians 2:9, Mark 11:24, Proverbs 16:3, Psalm 27:14, 1 Thessalonians 5:16-18.

• I am victor and never a victim. I will become all God has created me to be. I declare I walk in the blessings of the almighty God. I am filled with wisdom. I make good choices, have clear direction. I am blessed with creativity, with good ideas, with courage, with strength, and with ability.
Suggested verses: 1 John 5:4, 1 Corinthians 15:57, Luke 21:15, Psalm 18:32, Philippians 2:13.

• I declare right now that every negative word, every curse that has ever been spoken over me, is broken in the name of Jesus. I cancel all the generational curses that has bound my family for years. I speak of freedom, peace, and a new hope that comes from Christ alone. This is a new season in my life. Curses have been broken and blessings are on their way.
Suggested verses: Galatians 3:13, 2 Corinthians 5:17.

...all these things I ask and declare in Jesus' Name!

Notes

Notes

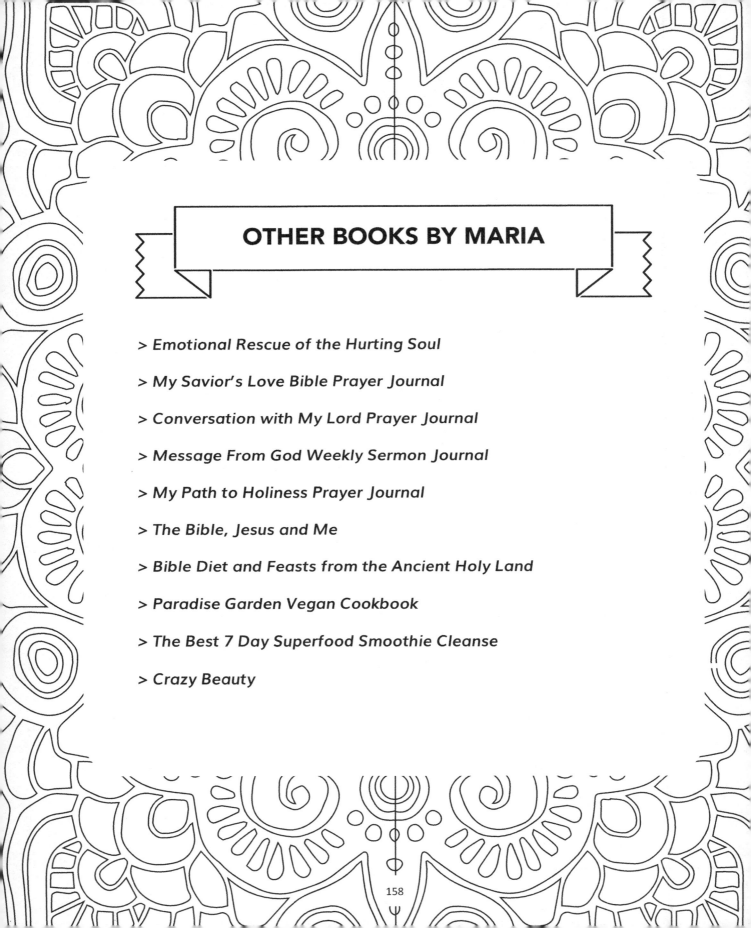

OTHER BOOKS BY MARIA

> *Emotional Rescue of the Hurting Soul*

> *My Savior's Love Bible Prayer Journal*

> *Conversation with My Lord Prayer Journal*

> *Message From God Weekly Sermon Journal*

> *My Path to Holiness Prayer Journal*

> *The Bible, Jesus and Me*

> *Bible Diet and Feasts from the Ancient Holy Land*

> *Paradise Garden Vegan Cookbook*

> *The Best 7 Day Superfood Smoothie Cleanse*

> *Crazy Beauty*

REFERENCES

• *Holy Bible:* All verses are quoted from the NIV or English Standard Version.

• *Excerpted from God's Chosen Fast:* A Spiritual and Practical Guide to Fasting by Arthur Wallis.

• Your Personal Guide to Prayer and Fasting by Dr. Bill Bright, 40 Day Guide to Fasting and Prayer.

• 21 Days of Prayer, Fasting, And Personal Devotion
http://fhchurch.org/wp-content/uploads/sites/2/2014/01/turningpoints_devos_2014web.pdf

• Effect of a 21 day Daniel Fast on metabolic and cardiovascular disease risk factors in men and women *https://www.ncbi.nlm.nih.gov/pmc/articles/PMC2941756/*

• The Daniel Fast by Susan Gregory.

• Healthy Ketosis & Intermittent Fasting *https://www.youtube.com/watch?v=3HxP2VXjtpQ:*

• Autophagy & Fasting *https://www.youtube.com/watch?v=XCvUf9WU4qI*

• Science of Fasting *https://www.youtube.com/watch?v=t1b08X-GvRs*

• Fasting for 72 Hours Can Reset Your Entire Immune System -
https://thesource.com/2018/11/21/fasting-for-72-hours-can-reset-your-entire-immune-system/

• How Intermittent Fasting Can Slow Aging, William Mair, Associate Professor At Harvard Chan School -
https://news.harvard.edu/gazette/story/2017/11/intermittent-fasting-may-be-center-of-increasing-lifespan/?utm_source=twitter&utm_medium=social&utm_campaign=hu-twitter-general

• Intermittent fasting vs daily calorie restriction for type 2 diabetes prevention: A review of human findings *https://www.sciencedirect.com/science/article/pii/S193152441400200X#bib24*

• Chronic Intermittent Fasting Improves Cognitive Functions and Brain Structures in Mice
https://journals.plos.org/plosone/article?id=10.1371/journal.pone.0066069

• Fasting weakens cancer in mice
https://news.usc.edu/29428/fasting-weakens-cancer-in-mice/

• Energy restriction and the prevention of breast cancer
https://www.ncbi.nlm.nih.gov/pubmed/22414375

• Water Fasting-The Clinical Effectiveness of Rebooting Your Body. Alan Goldhamer, Gustafson C. Integr Med (Encinitas). 2014 Jun;13(3):52-7.

• Bloomer, R. J., Kabir, M.M., Canale, R.E., Trepanowski, J.F., Marshall, K.E., Farney, T.M., & Hammond, K.G. (2010). Effect of a 21 day Daniel Fast on metabolic and cardiovascular disease risk factors in men and women. Lipids in Health and Disease, 9, 94-102. doi:10.1186/1476-511X-9-94.

• Campbell, T.C., & Campbell, T.M. (2004). The China study: Startling implications for diet, weight loss and long-term health. Dallas, TX: Benbella Books.

Made in the USA
Monee, IL
28 July 2023